LOOM AND SPINDLE

EARLY BOARDING HOUSE AND MILL SCENE OF LOWELL, MASSACHUSETTS

FROM *The New England Offering*, APRIL 1848

LOOM AND SPINDLE

OR

Life Among the Early Mill Girls

WITH A SKETCH OF

"THE LOWELL OFFERING" AND SOME
OF ITS CONTRIBUTORS

BY

HARRIET H. ROBINSON

INTRODUCTION
BY
JANE WILKINS PULTZ

PRESS PACIFICA
1976

A NOTE REGARDING THIS EDITION
This revised edition includes corrections which Harriet Robinson made in her own hand in the margins of her personal copy of "Loom and Spindle." Several redundant paragraphs of Mr. Thomas' letter, which repeated material already given in the text, have been deleted. The introduction to this edition replaces the one by the Honorable Carroll D. Wright in the 1898 edition.

INTRODUCTION

Loom and Spindle, a genuine American classic, has been lost to the public for too many years. Most of the remaining copies have been out of circulation, and can be found only in rare book collections or in special libraries. It is time that this rich, spirited history of the young women who went to work in the early cotton mills of Lowell, Massachusetts, be made available once more.

The author of these memoirs, Harriet Hanson Robinson, worked in the mills from the age of ten until her marriage at twenty-three; however, these were not years of constant labor. Until she was thirteen, the law required that she have three months off from work for schooling each year. We also know that she took some time off for high school work, and that she spent a long summer in Wentworth, N.H., in 1845. In 1835, the year Harriet first went to work in the mills, the pace of the machinery and labor was still relatively undemanding. By the time she left the mills in 1848, the industry's "speed-up" had led to intolerable conditions, which had, in turn, stimulated the formation of the active Lowell Female Labor Reform Association.

Most history books have maintained that by the second quarter of the nineteenth century the weaving of homespun cloth could not compete with the manufacture of cloth by machine, and that, therefore, young women were forced to go out of their homes and into the cotton mills to find employment. Historical research indicates, however, that the weaving of homespun was still an important part of the domestic economy at that time, and that the young women were not forced into the mills. Harriet's account shows that the young women were actively enticed into the mills because they were needed as a reliable source of labor by the mill owners, who were developing Lowell into the largest manufacturing center in the United States. The industrialists had tried hiring single men, and also whole families. Single men tended to leave in a short time for other jobs, or for the freedom of the frontier, and the families proved quarrelsome and difficult to supervise. When it occurred to the mill owners that the daughters of rural New England families could supply them with a good source of labor, they also realized that they would have to establish a suitable set of conditions to persuade the young women to leave their homes to go alone to work in Lowell.

Therefore, these astute "Lords of the Loom" cleverly created an atmosphere of propriety acceptable to both parents and daughters by setting up a system of boarding houses in which the residence of the female operatives was mandatory. These corporation houses were staffed by "mature *Christian* women," often, by widows. Furthermore, the male overseers who would be working directly with the operatives were described as "Sunday School teachers and deacons." Church attendance was required of all operatives according to mill rules. Once these arrangements had been put into practice, the mills were assured of a very good and cheap supply of labor.

Once the source of labor was relatively secure, the industry could apply itself to getting higher yields by a constant speed-up of machinery. This increase in production was not reflected in higher wages. Unfortunately, the writers of history books have tended to emphasize this exploitation of labor as the most important aspect of the early mill experience of these women workers. Merely focusing on the fact of economic exploitation, however, limits the scope of our understanding of what this early mill experience meant to the history of American women. The mill experience also had the effect of opening up new directions, releasing energies, and putting old stereotypes to the test. It put a new kind of power into these women's hands: cold, hard cash, to be spent at their discretion. Harriet Robinson has chosen to put her emphasis upon "new horizons" and not upon "exploitation." The story of what these young women did with their experience in the mills and in Lowell is what makes this memoir so unique and important.

In truth, life in Lowell was both exciting and difficult, satisfying and frustrating. For many who could make the choice, it was not the "best of all possible worlds" but the better of the two possibilities that young women had open to them: isolation in bucolic rural villages, or stimulation under the trying conditions of a noisy, busy city. Perhaps an excerpt of a letter written from one female operative to another will best set the stage for understanding the ambivalence in their actions and feelings:

"With a feeling which you can better imagine than I can describe as I announce to you the horrible tidings that I am once more a *factory girl!* yes, once more a factory girl seated in the short attic of a Lowell boarding house with half a dozen girls seated around me talking and reading and myself in the midst, trying to write to you . . . [After a three week vacation in Vermont] I returned home to enjoy a season of rest as I supposed, for my friends and my mother had almost persuaded me to stay at home during the fall and winter, but when I reached home I found a letter which informed me that Mr. Saunders was keeping my place for me and sent for me to come back as soon as I could! and after reading it my Lowell fever returned and, come I would, and come, I did, but now, "Ah! me. I rue the day" although I am not so homesick as I was a fortnight ago and just beginning to feel more resigned to my fate. I have been here for four weeks but have not had to work very hard for there are six girls of us and we have a fine time doing nothing . . . "

This letter was written at the height of the protests over working conditions by the Lowell Female Labor Reform League Association.

The one deficiency in Harriet's story is her silence on the great unionizing effort made by this Female Reform League, which had the support of at least a fifth of the workers. Sarah G. Bagely led this highly organized group of women operatives, protesting conditions in the mills during 1845–46. It was one of the first important efforts by laborers in America to improve their lot through organization.

There may be two reasons why Harriet did not mention the Female Reform League in her book. In the first place, she was away from Lowell during the summer of 1845, when there was an intense articulation of grievances and a strong organizing drive for members by the League. Also, she was allied by interest and friendship with the young women who wrote for the *Lowell Offering,* the famous monthly magazine written by the female operatives. The editor of this group, Harriet Farley, was often the target of attack by Sarah G. Bagley, who accused her, through the *Voice of Industry,* the weekly newspaper of the League, of being in the pay of the Corporation, and for being blind to the working conditions which they all shared in the mills. Whatever her stand was at that time, in the final analysis, this book is Harriet Robinson's testimony to her belief that working in the mill was a liberating rather than crippling experience. We can, however, only wish that she had included a commentary on the conflict of views between the *Lowell Offering* and the Lowell Female Labor Reform League Association.

Perusal of a collection of Harriet's papers reveals that her personal friends and acquaintances in the mills were young women with an amazing abundance of self-confidence and vitality. Many left the mills to teach, or to start their own schools, several went as missionaries to the Indians of the American West, one studied law and became an acting United States Treasurer, one went to Italy and became a well-known sculptor, and at least two founded libraries in their New Hampshire towns. Since many of Harriet's friends were contributors to the *Lowell Offering,* it is not surprising that they authored at least thirty-one books, four of them were editors of newspapers or magazines, and they published so many articles and stories in periodicals, ranging from Sunday School papers to the *Atlantic Monthly,* that it is impossible to estimate their number. Lucy Larcom, who also started in the mills at age ten, and who was a lifelong friend of Harriet Robinson, taught at Wheaton College, and was a well known poet in her day.

In Harriet Robinson's story of those early mill days, young women are, for the first time, a visible part of history, a discipline which has traditionally found only the adventures and contributions of young men worthy of study. This richly detailed account of the daily life in the mills, and of the later achievements of a small group of working-women who had been friends in their teens, is an important contribution to the history of nineteenth century America.

CONTENTS

CHAPTER I.

LOWELL SIXTY YEARS AGO.

"That wonderful city of spindles and looms,
And thousands of factory folk."

The life of a people or of a class is best illustrated by its domestic scenes, or by character sketches of the men and women who form a part of it. The historian is a species of mental photographer of the life and times he attempts to portray; he can no more give the whole history of events than the artist can, in detail, bring a whole city into his picture. And so, in this record of a life that is past, I can give but incomplete views of that long-ago faded landscape, views taken on the spot.

It is hardly possible to do this truthfully without bringing myself into the picture,—a solitary traveller revisiting the scenes of youth, and seeing with young eyes a city and a people living in almost Arcadian simplicity, at a time which, in view of the greatly changed conditions of factory labor, may well be called a lost Eden for that portion of our working-men and working-women.

Before 1836 the era of mechanical industry in New England had hardly begun, the industrial life of its people was yet in its infancy, and nearly every article in domestic use that is now made by the help of machinery was then "done by hand." It was, with few exceptions, a rural population, and the material for clothing was grown on the home-farm, and spun and woven by the women. Even in comparatively wealthy families, the sons were sent to college in suits of homespun, cut and made by the village seamstress, and every household was a self-producing and self-sustaining community. "Homespun was their only wear," homespun their lives.

There was neither railway, steamboat, telegraph, nor telephone, and direct communication was kept up by the lumbering stage-coach, or the slow-toiling canal, which tracked its sinuous way from town to city, and from State to State. The daily newspaper was almost unknown, and the "news of the day" was usually a week or so behind the times. Money was scarce, and most of the retail business was done by "barter"—so many eggs for a certain quantity of sugar, or so much butter or farm produce for tea, coffee, and other luxuries. The people had plenty to eat, for the land, though sterile, was well cultivated; but if the children wanted books, or a better education than the village school could give them, the farmer seldom had the means to gratify their wishes.

These early New Englanders lived in pastoral simplicity. They were moral, religious, and perhaps content. They could say with truth,—

> "We are the same things that our fathers have been,
> We see the same sights that our fathers have seen,
> We drink the same stream, we feel the same sun,
> And run the same course that our fathers have run."

Their lives had kept pace for so many years with the stage-coach and the canal that they thought, no doubt, if they thought about it at all, that they should crawl along in this way forever. But into this life there came an element that was to open a new era in the activities of the country.

This was the genius of mechanical industry, which would build the cotton-factory, set in motion the loom and the spinning-frame, call together an army of useful people, open wider fields of industry for men and (which was quite as important at that time) for women also. For hitherto woman had always been a money-*saving*, rather than a money-earning, member of the community, and her labor could command but small return. If she worked out as servant, or "help," her wages were from fifty cents to one dollar a week; if she went from house to house by the day to spin and weave, or as tailoress, she could get but seventy-five cents a week and her meals. As teacher her services were not in demand, and nearly all the arts, the professions, and even the trades and industries, were closed to her, there being, as late as 1840, only seven vocations, outside the home, into which the women of New England had entered.[1]

The Middlesex Canal was one of the earliest factors in New England enterprise. It began its course at Charlestown Mill-pond, and ended it at Lowell. It was completed in 1804, at the cost of $700,000, and was the first canal in the United States to transport both passengers and merchandise. Its charter was extinguished in 1859, in spite of all opposition, by a decision of the Supreme Court. And thus, in less than sixty years, this marvel of engineering skill, as it was then considered, which was projected to last for all time, was "switched off the track" by its successful rival, the Boston and Lowell Railroad, and, with the stage-coach and the turnpike road became a thing of the past.

The course of the old Middlesex Canal can still be traced, as a cow-path or a woodland lane, and in one place, which I have always kept in remembrance, very near the Somerville Station on the Western Division of the Boston and Maine Railroad, can still be seen a few decayed willows, nodding sleepily over its grass-grown channel and ridgy paths,—a reminder of those slow times when it took a long summer's day to travel the twenty-eight miles from Boston to Lowell.

The Boston and Lowell Railroad, probably the first in the United States, went into operation in 1835. I saw the first train that went out of Lowell, and there was great excitement over the event. People were gathered along the street near the *"deepot,"* discussing the great wonder; and we children stayed at home from school, or ran barefooted

---

[1] In addition to this, the corporation paid twenty-five cents a week to the boarding-house keeper, for each operative. But this sum was soon withdrawn, the girls were obliged to pay it themselves, and this was one of the grievances which caused the first strike among the Lowell factory operatives.

from our play, at the first "toot" of the whistle. As I stood on the sidewalk, I remember hearing those who stood near me disputing as to the probable result of this new attempt at locomotion. "The ingine never *can* start all them cars!" "She can, too." "She can't." "I don't believe a word of it." "She'll break down and kill everybody," was the cry.

But the engine did start, and the train came back, and the Boston and Lowell Railroad continued an independent line of travel for about the same number of years as its early rival; when, by the "irony of fate," its individuality was merged in that of a larger and more powerful organization,—the Boston and Maine Railroad, of which, in 1895, it became only a section or division. But let us not regret too much this accident of time, for who knows what will become of this enormous plant during the next fifty years, when our railways, perhaps, may be laid in the "unfeatured air."

The first factory for the manufacture of cotton cloth in the United States was erected in Beverly, Mass., in 1787, and in 1790 Samuel Slater established the cotton industry in Pawtucket, R.I.; but the first real effort to establish the enterprise was in Lowell, where a large wooden building was erected at the Wamesit Falls, on the Concord River, in 1813.

The history of Lowell, Mass., is not identical with that of other manufacturing places in New England, and for two reasons: first, because here were gathered together a larger number of factory people, and among them were the first who showed any visible sign of mental cultivation; and, second, because it was here that the practice of what was called "The Lowell factory system" went into operation, a practice which included the then new idea, that corporations should have souls, and should exercise a paternal influence over the lives of their operatives. As Dr. John O. Green of Lowell, in a letter to Lucy Larcom, said: "The design of the control of the boarding-houses and their inmates was one of the characteristics of the Lowell factory system, early incorporated therein by Mr. Francis Cabot Lowell and his brother-in-law, Patrick T. Jackson, who are entitled to all the credit of the acknowledged superiority of our early operatives."

Cotton-mills had also been started in Waltham, Mass., where the first power-loom went into operation in 1814; but, for lack of water-power, these could be carried on to a limited extent only. It was therefore resolved, by gentlemen interested, that the "plant" should be moved elsewhere, and water privileges were sought in Maine, New Hampshire, and in Massachusetts. Finally, Pawtucket Falls, on the Merrimack River, was selected, as a possible site where a large manufacturing town could be built up. Here land was bought, and the place, formerly a part of Chelmsford, set off in 1826, was named Lowell, after Francis Cabot Lowell, who, through his improvements, was practically the inventor of the power-loom, and the originator of the cotton-cloth manufacture as now carried on in America.

Kirk Boott, the agent of the first corporation, (as the mills, boarding-houses,—the whole plant was called), was a great potentate in the early history of Lowell, and exercised almost absolute power over the mill-people. Though not an Englishman, he had been educated in England, had imbibed the autocratic ideas of the mill-owners of the mother country, and many stories were told of his tyranny, or his "peculiarities," long after he ceased to be a resident.

Of his connection with the early history of Lowell, it is stated that, before the water-power was discovered there, he went as agent of the purchasers, to Gardiner, Me., and tried to buy of R.H. Gardiner, Esq., the great water privilege belonging to his estate. Mr. Gardiner would not sell, but was willing to lease it. Kirk Boott would not agree to this, or Lowell might now have been on the Kennebec in Maine. Then he came to Chelmsford, and saw the great Merrimack River and its possibilities, and set himself shrewdly to work to buy land on its banks, including the water-power. He represented to the simple farmers that he was going to raise fruit and wool, and they, knowing nothing of "mill privileges," believed him, and sold the greatest water-power in New England for almost nothing.

When they discovered his real design in buying the land, and the chance for making money that they had lost, they were angry enough. A song was made about it, and sung by everybody. It began thus:—

There came a young man from the old countree,
The Merrimack River he happened to see,
What a capital place for mills, quoth he,
   Ri-toot, ri-noot, ri-toot, ri-noot, riumpty, ri-tooten-a.

The next verse told how he swindled the farmers by inducing them to *sell* the water-power for nothing:—

And then these farmers so cute,
They *gave* all their lands and timber to Boott,
   Ri-toot, ri-noot, etc.

He was not popular, and the boys were so afraid of him that they would not go near him willingly, for many of them had known what it was to have his riding-whip come down on their backs. There is one still living who remembers how it felt. This old boy remembers that one Fourth of July Kirk Boott raised the English and American flags over his house, with the Stars and Stripes *under* the English colors; he would not change them at the suggestion of an indignant mob who had gathered, and they did it for him. Kirk Boott's house and garden were located on the spot where the Boott Corporation now stands. The house was a very fine mansion and stood near the river, and the garden was a wonder to everybody, fruit and flowers were brought to such perfection. So he did fulfil his promise after a sort to the former owners of the land, for he raised fruit on some of it, and the wool he raised, metaphorically, and pulled (as the song intimated) over the eyes of the deluded farmers.

The Merrimack Manufacturing Company was incorporated in 1822, a factory was built, and the first cotton cloth was made in 1823. It was coarse in texture,—the kind that might be used to "shoot pease through,"—though it was not sleazy, but thick and firm, something like thin sail-cloth, and it costs "two and threepence" (thirty-seven and one-half cents) a yard.

The first calico printing done in Lowell was on the Merrimack Corporation, and the prints were of very poor texture and color. The groundwork was madder, and there was a white spot in it for a figure; it cost about thirty cents a yard. This madder-color was the product of an extensive cowyard in the vicinity of the print-works, and the prints were "warranted not to fade."

I had a gown of this material, and it proved a garb of humiliation, for the white spots washed out, cloth and all, leaving me covered with eyelet-holes. This so amused my witty brother that, whenever I wore it, he accused me of being more "holy than righteous." Dyers and calico printers were soon sent for from England, and a long low block on the Merrimack Corporation was built for their accommodation and called the "English Row." When they arrived from the old country they were not satisfied with the wages, which were not according to the agreement, and they would not go to work, but left the town with their families in a large wagon with a band of music. Terms were made with them, however, and they returned, and established in Lowell the art of calico printing.

The "Print Works" was a great mystery in its early days. It had its secrets, and it was said that no stranger was allowed to enter certain rooms, for fear that the art would be stolen. The first enduring color in print was an indigo blue. This was the groundwork, and a minute white spot sprinkled over it made the goods lively and pretty. It wore like "iron," and its success was the first step toward the high standard in the market once held by the "Merrimack Print."

Before 1840, the foreign element in the factory population was almost an unknown quantity. The first imigrants to come to Lowell were from England. The Irishman soon followed; but not for many years did the Frenchman, Italian, and German come to take possession of the cotton-mills. The English were of the artisan class, but the Irish came as "hewers of wood and drawers of water." The first Irishwomen to work in the Lowell mills were usually scrubbers and waste-pickers. They were always good-natured, and when excited used their own language; the little mill-children learned many of the words (which all seemed to be joined together like compound words), and these mites would often answer back, in true Hibernian fashion. These women, as a rule, wore peasant cloaks, red or blue, made with hoods and several capes, in summer (as they told the children), to "kape cool," and in winter to "kape warrum." They were not intemperate, nor "bitterly poor." They earned good wages, and they and their children, especially their children, very soon adapted themselves to their changed conditions of life, and became as "good as anybody."

To show the close connection in family descent of the artisan and the artist, at least in the line of color, it may be said here that a grandson of one of the first blue-dyers in this country is one of the finest American marine painters, and exhibited pictures at the World's Columbian Exposition of 1893.

In 1832 the factory population of Lowell was divided into four classes. The agents of the corporations were the aristocrats, not because of their wealth, but on account of the office they held, which was one of great responsibility, requiring, as it did, not only some knowledge of business, but also a certain tact in managing, or utilizing the great number of operatives so as to secure the best return for their labor. The agent was also something of an autocrat, and there was no appeal from his decision in matters affecting the industrial interests of those who were employed on his corporation.

The agents usually lived in large houses, not too near the boarding-houses, surrounded by beautiful gardens which seemed like Paradise to some of the home-sick girls, who, as they came from their work in the noisy mill, could look with longing eyes into the sometimes open gate in the high fence, and be reminded afresh of their pleasant country homes. And a glimpse of one handsome woman, the wife of an agent, reading by an astral lamp in the early evening, has always been remembered by one young girl, who looked forward to the time when she, too, might have a parlor of her own, lighted by an astral lamp!

The second class were the overseers, a sort of gentry,

ambitious mill-hands who had worked up from the lowest grade of factory labor; and they usually lived in the end-tenements of the blocks, the short connected rows of houses in which the operatives were boarded. However, on one corporation, at least, there was a block devoted exclusively to the overseers, and one of the wives, who had been a factory girl, put on so many airs that the wittiest of her former work-mates fastened the name of "Puckersville" to the whole block where the overseers lived. It was related of one of these quondam factory girls, that, with some friends, she once re-visited the room in which she used to work, and, to show her genteel friends her ignorance of her old surroundings, she turned to the overseer, who was with the party, and pointing to some wheels and pulleys over her head, she said, "What's them things up there?"

The third class were the operatives, and were all spoken of as "girls" or "men;" and the "girls," either as a whole, or in part, are the subject of this volume.

The fourth class, lords of the spade and the shovel, by whose constant labor the building of the great factories was made possible, and whose children soon became valuable operatives, lived at first on what was called the "Acre," a locality near the present site of the North Grammar schoolhouse. Here, clustered around a small stone Catholic Church, were hundreds of little shanties, in which they dwelt with their wives and numerous children. Among them were sometimes found disorder and riot, for they had brought with them from the *ould counthrey* their feuds and quarrels, and the "Bloody Fardowners" and the "Corkonians" were torn by intestinal strife. The boys of both these factions agreed in fighting the "damned Yankee boys," who represented to them both sides of the feud on occasion; and I have seen many a pitched battle fought, all the way from the Tremont Corporation (then an open field) to the North Grammar schoolhouse, before we girls could be allowed to pursue our way in peace.

We were obliged to go to school with our champions,

the boys, for we did not dare to go alone. These "Acreites" respected one or two of us from our relationship to the "bullies," as some of the fighting leaders of our boys were called; and when caught alone by Acreites coming home from school, we have been in terror of our lives, till we heard some of them say, in a language used by all sides, air-o-there owes-o-gose e-o-the ooly-o-boos' ister-o-see. (There goes the bully's sister.) This language was called Hog Latin by the boys; but it is found in one of George Borrows' books, as a specimen of the Rommany or gypsy language. These fights were not confined to the boys on each side; after mill-hours the men joined in the fray, and evenings that should have been better employed were spent in carrying on this senseless warfare. The authorities interfered, and prevented these raids of the Acreites upon the school-children, and the warfare was kept within their own domain. It lasted after this for more than ten years, and was ended by the "bloody battle" of Suffolk Bridge, in which a young boy was killed.

The agents were paid only fair salaries, the overseers generally two dollars a day, and the help all earned good wages. By this it will be seen that there were no very rich persons in Lowell, nor were there any "suffering poor," since every man, woman, and child, (over ten years of age) could get work, and was paid according to the work each was capable of doing.

The richest young lady of my time was the daughter of a deceased mill-owner; her income, it was said, was six hundred dollars a year! And many of the factory girls made from six to ten dollars a week! out of this, to be sure, they paid their board, which was one dollar and twenty-five cents a week.[1]

By this it will be seen that there could not have been much aristocracy of wealth; but (as in most manufacturing cities to-day), there was a class feeling, which divided

---

[1] In addition to this, the corporation paid twenty-five cents a week to the boarding-housekeeper, for each operative. But this sum was soon withdrawn, the girls were obliged to pay it themselves, and this was one of the grievances which caused the first strike among the Lowell factory operatives.

the people, though not their interests. For, as has been
said, the corporation guarded well the interests of its
employees; and as the mill-hands looked to the factories
for their support, they worked as one man (and one woman) to help increase the growing prosperity of the city,
which had given to them a new and permanent means
of earning a livelihood.

The history of Lowell gives a good illustration of the
influence of woman, as an independent class, upon the
growth of a town or a community.

As early as 1836, ten years after its incorporation, Lowell
began to show what the early mill girls and boys could
do towards the material prosperity of a great city. It num-
bered over 17,000 inhabitants,—an increase of over 15,000
during that time.

In 1843 over one-half of the depositors in the Lowell
Institution for Savings were mill-girls, and over one-
third of the whole sum deposited belonged to them,—in
round numbers, $101,992; and the new-made city showed
unmistakable signs of becoming, what it was afterwards
called, the "Manchester of America." But the money of
the operatives alone could not have so increased the growth
and social importance of a city or a locality. It was the result, as well, of the successful operation of the early factory system, managed by men who were wise enough to
consider the physical, moral, and mental needs of those
who were the source of their wealth.

Free co-educational schools were established in Lowell
as early as 1830–1832, and a rule was made by the
several corporations that every child under fourteen
should attend them three months in the year.

Master Hills taught the North Grammar School, after
it occupied its present site. I remember him in 1835;
and I pause when I think of this teacher, and wonder if,
in some other sphere, he remembers whipping a little girl
to overcome her persistent denials of an accusation made
against her, thereby forcing her to tell a lie. She was
accused by one of her schoolmates of taking a one cent
multiplication table from her desk, and tearing it in two.
For this slight offence, he, a strong man, unheeding her

denials of the charge, with a heavy strap, struck with his whole strength on the tender palm of the little hand of a child of scarcely ten years. He punished her till she could not see, for pain and terror, and then she gave in, *whipped into a lie,* and said she did it.

The punishment over she staggered to her seat, thinking that at last it was all over. But the end was not yet, for she had to learn by this early experience that one is but the beginning of a sum, and that she must tell many lies and keep on telling them, in order to maintain her position. Her little schoolmates said, "Why did you not say sooner that you did it, and save yourself all that whipping?" She could not tell them the truth, for they would not believe her. Her dear mother said, "If you wanted another multiplication table, why did you not ask me for one?" But she could not even confess the truth to her. Her good aunt accosted her with, "You sinner! do you not know what becomes of liars?" She could not justify herself to avert *that* awful fate, and so she went on throwing out lie after lie (a heavy ballast), to save herself and to maintain her standing as a liar, till she was heartily sick of the whole matter, and wished that she had stuck to the truth, even if the master had killed her.

I have known Master Hills to go secretly behind a boy, who was playing at his desk, and strike him with a heavy strap across the back. Whipping was an every-day occurrence, and was done before all the children during school hours. A boy was made to lie across a chair, and was whipped in that position—not always through his clothing. Let us charitably hope that this cruel treatment of children was the fault of the times and of the arbitrary rule that was thought necessary to govern a community in those days. The day of children's rights had not yet dawned.

Master Jacob Graves followed Mr. Hills, and he was the first teacher that I remember who used moral suasion, and instilled into our minds what honor among children meant. He taught us to be truthful for truth's sake, his rule was mild and pleasant, he never punished with the rod, and his kind, remonstrating voice was more powerful than any whipping. In later life, many of his scholars sorrowed with him in his misfortunes, and now his memory lives in their hearts, a tender and pleasant recollection. The first church edifice built in Lowell was St. Anne's. It was built under Kirk Boott's reign; and, without regard to the difference of the religious opinions of the operatives, the Episcopal form of service was adopted. Every operative on the Merrimack corporation was obliged to pay thirty-seven and a half cents a month toward the support of this church. This was considered unjust by the help, many of whom were "dissenters," and they complained so loudly at the extortion, which was not in the contract, that the tax was soon discontinued.

The Freewill Baptist Church was built largely of money belonging to over one hundred factory girls, who were induced by Elder Thurston's promises of large interest to draw their money from the savings-bank, and place it in his hands. These credulous operatives did not even receive the interest of their money, but, believing in him as an elder of the church, they were persuaded, even a second time, to let him have their savings. This building has had a curious and eventful history, "from grave to gay, from lively to severe." According to Mr. Cowley's history of Lowell, nothing had succeeded in it; and, to a believer in retributive justice, it would seem as if even the building deserved to be under a ban till those hard earnings were restored. The money wasted there represents so much of lost opportunity of education, lost means of comfort and maintenance, lost ability to keep or help the dear ones at home.

Early in the history of Lowell, Universalism became popular, and a large congregation, mostly young people, were soon gathered. This quite frightened those of certain other sects, and their ministers preached openly against the new doctrine; discussions and controversies were rife, and whether there was a hell or not, was the chief topic of the day among the factory people. That there was not was, of course, the more agreeable, and, with the fearless ones, the more popular side. There was a very benighted idea in the minds of many as to what this new religion really was, and "Infidel," and "Atheist," were the names applied by other denominations. Doctrinal feeling was strong, and young people who went with the "awful Universalists" received no favor from the other sects. The Unitarians also came under the ban, but the Universalists were the more condemned; and the good work they tried to do was hindered in more than one direction by this unchristian persecution.

As a matter of local history, it may be well to add here, that in its earlier days Lowell furnished quite a number of distinguished men. Among its physicians may be mentioned Dr. Elisha Bartlett, who was widely known as a man of scientific culture and of many accomplishments; the Daltons, father and sons, later of Boston; and Dr. Gilman Kimball, the celebrated surgeon. Lieutenant-Governor Huntington also practised medicine there, as did Dr. John O. Greene, the antiquary. Wendell Phillips was in a law-office, and John Nesmith, manufacturer, was lieutenant-governor during a part of Governor Andrew's term of office. In Freesoil days John G. Whittier edited a paper there, and John H. Warland and H. Hastings Weld were in the same profession. Colonel William Schouler began editorial life in Lowell, assisted by William S. Robinson ("Warrington"), who went from Concord, Mass., in 1842. Mr. Robinson also published *The Lowell American,* one of the first Freesoil papers, from 1849 to 1854. William Worthen, of the firm of D. Appleton & Co. of New York, was formerly of Lowell, a Worthen being one of the founders of the city. Warren Colburn of "Colburn's Sequel," the mathematician, was agent of the Merrimack Mills. John P. Robinson, who was so severely lampooned by the poet Lowell ("John P. Robinson, he"), moved to Lowell from Dover early in life. The Hon. Gustavus Vasa Fox, once Assistant Secretary of the Navy, lived with his mother on the Tremont Corporation. Major-General B.F. Butler was one of its most widely known citizens. Henry F. Durant, the founder of Wellesley College, studied law in the office of his father, William Smith, and Major-General N.P. Banks was bobbin-boy, and afterward editor there. The late Rev. W.H. Cudworth, and J.W. Hanson, D.D., now of Chicago, were cousins and Lowell boys, and were both

chaplains of Massachusetts regiments during the Civil
War. James McNeil Whistler, the painter, was born in
Lowell, in 1834.

Lowell has never been a book-publishing place; but it
is a curious fact that the first American edition of Hay-
ward's translation of "Faust" was published there in 1840
by Daniel Bixby, afterward of New York.

CHAPTER II.

CHILD-LIFE IN THE LOWELL COTTON-MILLS

IN attempting to describe the life and times of the early mill-girls, it has seemed best for me to write my story in the first person; not so much because my own experience is of importance, as that it is, in some respects, typical of that of many others who lived and worked with me.

Our home was in Boston, in Leverett Court, now Cotting Street, where I was born the year the corner-stone was laid for the Bunker Hill Monument, as my mother told me always to remember. We lived there until I was nearly seven years of age, and, although so young, I can remember very vividly scenes and incidents which took place at that time. We lived under the shadow of the old jail (near where Wall Street now runs), and we children used to hear conversation, not meant for small ears, between the prisoners and the persons in the court who came there to see them.

All the land on which the North Union Station now stands, with the railway lines connected with it, and also the site of many of the streets, particularly Lowell Street, was then a part of the Mill-pond, or was reclaimed from the Bay. The tide came in at the foot of Leverett Court, and we could look across the water and see the sailing vessels coming and going. There the down-east wood-coasters landed their freight; many a time I have gone "chipping" there, and once a generous young skipper offered me a stick of wood, which I did not dare to take.

In 1831, under the shadow of a great sorrow, which had made her four children fatherless,—the oldest but seven years of age,—my mother was left to struggle alone; and, although she tried hard to earn bread enough to fill our hungry mouths, she could not do it, even with the help of kind friends. And so it happened that one of her more wealthy neighbors, who had looked with longing eyes on the one little daughter of the family, offered to adopt me. But my mother, who had had a hard experience in her youth in living amongst strangers, said, "No; while I have one meal of victuals a day, I will not part with my children." I always remembered this speech because of the word "victuals," and I wondered for a long time what this good old Bible word meant.

My father was a carpenter, and some of his fellow-workmen helped my mother to open a little shop, where she sold small stores, candy, kindling-wood, and so on, but there was no great income from this, and we soon became poorer than ever. Dear me! I can see the small shop now, with its jars of striped candy, its loaves of bread, the room at the back where we all lived, and my oldest brother (now a "D.D.") sawing the kindling-wood which we sold to the neighbors.

That was a hard, cold winter; and for warmth's sake my mother and her four children all slept in one bed, two at the foot and three at the head,—but her richer neighbor could not get the little daughter; and, contrary to all the modern notions about hygiene, we were a healthful and a robust brood. We all, except the baby, went to school every day, and Saturday afternoons I went to a charity school to learn to sew. My mother had never complained of her poverty in our hearing, and I had accepted the conditions of my life with a child's trust, knowing nothing of the relative difference between poverty and riches. And so I went to the sewing-school, like any other little girl who was taking lessons in sewing and not as a "charity child;" until a certain day when something was said by one of the teachers, about me, as a "poor little girl,"—a thoughtless remark, no doubt, such as may be said to-day in "charity schools." When I went home I told my mother that the teacher said I was *poor,* and she replied in her sententious manner, "You need not go there again."

Shortly after this my mother's widowed sister, Mrs. Angeline Cudworth, who kept a factory boarding-house in Lowell, advised her to come to that city. She secured a

house for her, and my mother, with her little brood and
her few household belongings, started for the new factory town.

We went by the canal-boat, The Governor Sullivan, and
a long and tiresome day it was to the weary mother and
her four active children, though the children often varied
the scene by walking on the tow-path under the Lombardy
poplars, riding on the gates when the locks were swung
open, or buying glasses of water at the stopping-places
along the route.

When we reached Lowell, we were carried at once to
my aunt's house, whose generous spirit had well provided
for her hungry relations; and we children were led into
her kitchen, where, on the longest and whitest of tables,
lay, oh, so many loaves of bread!

After our feast of loaves we walked with our mother
to the Tremont Corporation, where we were to live, and
at the old No. 5 (which imprint is still legible over the door),
in the first block of tenements then built, I began my life
among factory people. My mother kept forty boarders,
most of them men, mill-hands, and she did all her housework, with what help her children could give her between
schools; for we all, even the baby three years old, were
kept at school. My part in the housework was to wash the
dishes, and I was obliged to stand on a cricket in order to
reach the sink!

My mother's boarders were many of them young men,
and usually farmers' sons. They were almost invariably
of good character and behavior, and it was a continual
pleasure for me and my brothers to associate with them.
I was treated like a little sister, never hearing a word or
seeing a look to remind me that I was not of the same sex
as my brothers. I played checkers with them, sometimes
"beating," and took part in their conversation, and it
never came into my mind that they were not the same as
so many "girls." A good object-lesson for one who was in
the future to maintain, by voice and pen, her belief in the
equality of the sexes!

I had been to school constantly until I was about ten

years of age, when my mother, feeling obliged to have help in her work besides what I could give, and also needing the money which I could earn, allowed me, at my urgent request (for I wanted to earn *money* like the other little girls), to go to work in the mill. I worked first in the spinning-room as a "doffer." The doffers were the very youngest girls, whose work was to doff, or take off, the full bobbins, and replace them with the empty ones.

I can see myself now, racing down the alley, between the spinning-frames, carrying in front of me a bobbin-box bigger than I was. These mites had to be very swift in their movements, so as not to keep the spinning-frames stopped long, and they worked only about fifteen minutes in every hour. The rest of the time was their own, and when the overseer was kind they were allowed to read, knit, or even to go outside the mill-yard to play.

Some of us learned to embroider in crewels, and I still have a lamb worked on cloth, a relic of those early days, when I was first taught to improve my time in the good old New England fashion. When not doffing, we were often allowed to go home, for a time, and thus we were able to help our mothers in their housework. We were paid two dollars a week; and how proud I was when my turn came to stand up on the bobbin-box, and write my name in the paymaster's book, and how indignant I was when he asked me if I could "write." "Of course I can," said I, and he smiled as he looked down on me.

The working-hours of all the girls extended from five o'clock in the morning until seven in the evening, with one-half hour for breakfast and for dinner. Even the doffers were forced to be on duty nearly fourteen hours a day, and this was the greatest hardship in the lives of these children. For it was not until 1842 that the hours of labor for children under twelve years of age were limited to ten per day; but the "ten-hour law" itself was not passed until long after some of these little doffers were old enough to appear before the legislative committee on the subject, and plead, by their presence, for a reduction of the hours of labor.

I do not recall any particular hardship connected with this life, except getting up so early in the morning, and to this habit, I never was, and never shall be, reconciled, for it has taken nearly a lifetime for me to make up the sleep lost at that early age. But in every other respect it was a pleasant life. We were not hurried any more than was for our good, and no more work was required of us than we were able easily to do.

Most of us children lived at home, and we were well fed, drinking both tea and coffee, and eating substantial meals (besides luncheons) three times a day. We had very happy hours with the older girls, many of whom treated us like babies, or talked in a motherly way, and so had a good influence over us. And in the long winter evenings, when we could not run home between the doffings, we gathered in groups and told each other stories, and sung the old-time songs our mothers had sung, such as "Barbara Allen," "Lord Lovell," "Captain Kid," "Hull's Victory," and sometimes a hymn.

Among the ghost stories I remember some that would delight the hearts of the "Society for Psychical Research." The more imaginative ones told of what they had read in fairy books, or related tales of old castles and distressed maidens; and the scene of their adventures was sometimes laid among the foundation stones of the new mill, just building.

And we told each other of our little hopes and desires, and what we meant to do when we grew up. For we had our aspirations; and one of us, who danced the "shawl dance," as she called it, in the spinning-room alley, for the amusement of her admiring companions, discussed seriously with another little girl the scheme of their running away together, and joining the circus. Fortunately, there was a grain of good sense lurking in the mind of this gay little lassie, with the thought of the mother at home, and the scheme was not carried out.

There was another little girl, whose mother was suffering with consumption, and who went out of the mill almost every forenoon, to buy and cook oysters, which she brought in hot, for her mother's luncheon. The mother soon went to her rest, and the little daughter, after tasting the first bitter experience of life, followed her. Dear Lizzie Osborne! little sister of my child-soul, such friendship as ours is not often repeated in after life! Many pathetic stories might be told of these little fatherless mill-children, who worked near their mothers, and who went hand in hand with them to and from the mill.

I cannot tell how it happened that some of us knew about the English factory children, who, it was said, were treated so badly, and were even whipped by their cruel overseers. But we did know of it, and used to sing, to a doleful little tune, some verses called, "The Factory Girl's Last Day." I do not remember it well enough to quote it as written, but have refreshed my memory by reading it lately in Robert Dale Owen's writings:—

"THE FACTORY GIRL'S LAST DAY.

"'Twas on a winter morning,
 The weather wet and wild,
Two hours before the dawning
 The father roused his child,
Her daily morsel bringing,
 The darksome room he paced,
And cried, 'The bell is ringing—
 My hapless darling, haste!'

The overlooker met her
 As to her frame she crept;
And with his thong he beat her,
 And cursed her when she wept.
It seemed as she grew weaker,
 The threads the oftener broke,
The rapid wheels ran quicker,
 And heavier fell the stroke."

The song goes on to tell the sad story of her death while her "pitying comrades" were carrying her home to die, and ends:—

"That night a chariot passed her,
 While on the ground she lay;
The daughters of her master,
 An evening visit pay.

> Their tender hearts were sighing,
> As negroes' wrongs were told,
> While the white slave was dying
> Who gained her father's gold."

In contrast with this sad picture, we thought of ourselves as well off, in our cosey corner of the mill, enjoying ourselves in our own way, with our good mothers and our warm suppers awaiting us when the going-out bell should ring.

Holidays came when repairs to the great mill-wheel were going on, or some late spring freshet caused the shutting down of the mill; these were well improved. With what freedom we enjoyed those happy times! My summer playhouse was the woodshed, which my mother always had well filled; how orderly and with what precision the logs were sawed and piled with the smooth ends outwards! The catacombs of Paris reminded me of my old playhouse. And here, in my castle of sawed wood, was my vacation retreat, where, with my only and beloved wooden doll, I lunched on slices of apple cut in shape so as to represent what I called "German half-moon cakes." I piled up my bits of crockery with sticks of cinnamon to represent candy, and many other semblances of things, drawn from my mother's housekeeping stores.

The yard which led to the shed was always green, and here many half-holiday duties were performed. We children were expected to scour all the knives and forks used by the forty men-boarders, and my brothers often bought themselves off by giving me some trifle, and I was left alone to do the whole. And what a pile of knives and forks it was! But it was no task, for did I not have the open yard to work in, with the sky over me, and the green grass to stand on, as I scrubbed away at my "stent"? I don't know why I did not think such long tasks a burden, nor of my work in the mill as drudgery. Perhaps it was because I *expected* to do my part towards helping my mother to get our living, and had never heard her complain of the hardships of her life.

On other afternoons I went to walk with a playmate, who, like myself, was full of romantic dreams, along the banks of the Merrimack River, where the Indians had still their tents, or on Sundays, to see the "new converts" baptized. These baptizings in the river were very common, as the tanks in the churches were not considered *apostolic* by the early Baptists of Lowell.

Sometimes we rambled by the "race-way" or mill-race, which carried the water into the flume of the mill, along whose inclining sides grew wild roses, and the "rock-loving columbine;" and we used to listen to see if we could hear the blue-bells ring,—this was long before either of us had read a line of poetry.

The North Grammar school building stood at the base of a hilly ridge of rocks, down which we coasted in winter, and where in summer, after school-hours, we had a little cave, where we sometimes hid, and played that we were robbers; and together we rehearsed the dramatic scenes in "Alonzo and Melissa," "The Children of the Abbey," or the "Three Spaniards;" we were turned out of doors with Amanda, we exclaimed "Heavens!" with Melissa, and when night came on we fled from our playhouse pursued by the dreadful apparition of old Don Padilla through the dark windings of those old rocks, towards our commonplace home. "Ah!" as some writer has said, "if one could only add the fine imagination of those early days to the knowledge and experience of later years, what books might not be written!"

Our home amusements were very original. We had no toys, except a few homemade articles or devices of our own. I had but a single doll, a wooden-jointed thing, with red cheeks and staring black eyes. Playing-cards were tabooed, but my elder brother (the incipient D.D.), who had somehow learned the game of high-low-jack, set about making a pack. The cards were cut out of thick yellow pasteboard, the spots and figures were made in ink, and, to disguise their real character, the names of the suits were changed. Instead of hearts, diamonds, spades and clubs, they were called charity, love, benevolence, and faith. The pasteboard was so thick that all together the cards made a pile at least two or three feet high, and they had to be shuffled in sections! He taught my second

brother and me the game of high-low-jack; and, with de-
lightful secrecy, as often as we could steal away, we played
in the attic, keeping the cards hidden, between whiles,
in an old hair trunk. In playing the game we got along very
well with the names of the face-cards,—the "queen of
charity," the "king of love," and so on; but the "ten-spot
of faith," and particularly the "two-spot of benevolence"
(we had never heard of the "deuce") was too much for
our sense of humor, and almost spoiled the "rigor of the
game."

I was a "little doffer" until I became old enough to earn
more money; then I tended a spinning-frame for a little
while; and after that I learned, on the Merrimack corporation, to be a drawing-in girl, which was considered one
of the most desirable employments, as about only a dozen
girls were needed in each mill. We drew in, one by one,
the threads of the warp, through the harness and the reed,
and so made the beams ready for the weaver's loom. I still
have the two hooks I used so long, companions of many
a dreaming hour, and preserve them as the "badge of all
my tribe" of drawing-in girls.

It may be well to add that, although so many changes
have been made in mill-work, during the last fifty years,
by the introduction of machinery, this part of it still continues to be done by hand, and the drawing-in girl—I saw
her last winter, as in my time—still sits on her high stool,
and with her little hook patiently draws in the thousands
of threads, one by one.

CHAPTER III.

THE LITTLE MILL-GIRL'S ALMA MATER.

THE education of a child is an all-around process, and he or she owes only a part of it to school or college training. The child to whom neither college nor school is open must find his whole education in his surroundings, and in the life he is forced to lead. As the cotton-factory was the means of the early schooling of so large a number of men and women, who, without the opportunity thus afforded, could not have been mentally so well developed, I love to call it their *Alma Mater*. For, without this incentive to labor, this chance to earn extra money and to use it in their own way, their influence on the times, and also, to a certain extent, on modern civilization, would certainly have been lost.

I had been to school quite constantly until I was nearly eleven years of age, and then, after going into the mill, I went to some of the evening schools that had been established, and which were always well filled with those who desired to improve their scant education, or to supplement what they had learned in the village school or academy. Here might often be seen a little girl puzzling over her sums in Colburn's Arithmetic, and at her side another "girl" of fifty poring over her lesson in Pierpont's National Reader.

Some of these schools were devoted to special studies. I went to a geography school, where the lessons were repeated in unison in a monotonous sing-song tone, like this: "Lake Winni*peg!* Lake Winni*peg!* Lake Titi*caca!* Lake Titi*caca! Mem*phre*ma*gog! *Mem*phre*ma*gog!" and also to a school where those who fancied they had thoughts were taught by Newman's Rhetoric to express them in writing. In this school, the relative position of the subject and the predicate was not always well taught by the master; but never to mix a metaphor or to confuse a simile was a lesson he firmly fixed in the minds of his pupils.

As a result of this particular training, I may say here, that, while I do not often mix metaphors, I am to this day almost as ignorant of what is called "grammar" as Dean Swift, who, when he went up to answer for his degree, said he "could not tell a subject from a predicate;" or even James Whitcomb Riley, who said he "would not know a nominative if he should meet it on the street."

The best practical lesson in the proper use of at least one grammatical sentence was given to me by my elder brother (not two years older than I) one day, when I said, "I done it." "You done it!" said he, taking me by the shoulder and looking me severely in the face, "Don't you ever let me hear you say *I done it* again, unless you can use *have* or *had* before it." I also went to singing-school, and became a member of the church choir, and in this way learned many beautiful hymns that made a lasting impression on the serious part of my nature.

The discipline our work brought us was of great value. We were obliged to be in the mill at just such a minute, in every hour, in order to doff our full bobbins and replace them with empty ones. We went to our meals and returned at the same hour every day. We worked and played at regular intervals, and thus our hands became deft, our fingers nimble, our feet swift, and we were taught daily habits of regularity and of industry; it was, in fact, a sort of manual training or industrial school.

Some of us were fond of reading, and we read all the books we could borrow. One of my mother's boarders, a farmer's daughter from "the State of Maine," had come to Lowell to work, for the express purpose of getting books, usually novels, to read, that she could not find in her native place. She read from two to four volumes a week; and we children used to get them from the circulating library, and return them, for her. In exchange for this, she allowed us to read her books, while she was at work in the mill; and what a scurrying there used to be home from school, to get the first chance at the new book!

It was as good as a fortune to us, and all for six and a quarter cents a week! In this way I read the novels of

Richardson, Madame D'Arblay, Fielding, Smollett, Cooper, Scott, Captain Marryatt, and many another old book not included in Mr. Ruskin's list of "one hundred good books." Passing through the alembic of a child's pure mind, I am not now conscious that the reading of the doubtful ones did me any lasting harm. But I should add that I do not advise such indiscriminate reading among young people, and there is no need of it, since now there are so many good books, easy of access, which have not the faults of those I was obliged to read. Then, there was no choice. Today, the best of reading, for children and young people, can be found everywhere.

"Lalla Rookh" was the first poem I ever read, and it awoke in me, not only a love of poetry, but also a desire to try my own hand at verse-making.

And so the process of education went on, and I, with many another "little doffer," had more than one chance to nibble at the root of knowledge. I had been to school for three months in each year, until I was about thirteen years old, when my mother, who was now a little better able to do without my earnings, sent me to the Lowell High School regularly for two years, adding her constant injunction, "Improve your mind, try and be somebody." There I was taught a little of everything, including French and Latin; and I may say here that my "little learning," in French at least, proved "a dangerous thing," as I had reason to know some years later, when I tried to speak my book-French in Paris, for it might as well have been Choctaw, when used as a means of oral communication with the natives of that fascinating city.

The Lowell high school, in about 1840, was kept in a wooden building over a butcher's shop, but soon afterwards the new high school, still in use, was provided, and it was co-educational. How well I remember some of the boys and girls, and I recall them with pleasure if not with affection. I could name them now, and have noted with pride their success in life. A few are so high above the rest that one would be surprised to know that they received the principal part of their school education in that little high school room over the butcher's shop.

I left the high school when fifteen years of age, my school education completed; though after that I took private lessons in German, drawing, and dancing! About this time my elder brother and I made up our minds that our mother had worked hard long enough, and we prevailed on her to give up keeping boarders. This she did, and while she remained in Lowell we supported the home by our earnings. I was obliged to have my breakfast before daylight in the winter. My mother prepared it over night, and while I was cooking and eating it I read such books as Stevens's "Travels" in Yucatan and in Mexico, Tasso's "Jerusalem Delivered," and "Lights and Shadows of Scottish Life." My elder brother was the clerk in the counting-room of the Tremont Corporation, and the agent, Mr. Charles L. Tilden,—whom I thank, wherever he may be,—allowed him to carry home at night, or over Sunday, any book that might be left on his (the agent's) desk; by this means I read many a beloved volume of poetry, late into the night and on Sunday. Longfellow, in particular, I learned almost by heart, and so retentive is the young memory that I can repeat, even now, whole poems.

I read and studied also at my work; and as this was done by the job, or beam, if I chose to have a book in my lap, and glance at it at intervals, or even write a bit, nothing was lost to the "corporation."

Lucy Larcom, in her "New England Girlhood," speaks of the windows in the mill on whose sides were pasted newspaper clippings, which she calls "window gems." It was very common for the spinners and weavers to do this, as they were not allowed to read books openly in the mill; but they brought their favorite "pieces" of poetry, hymns, and extracts, and pasted them up over their looms or frames, so that they could glance at them, and commit them to memory. We little girls were fond of reading these clippings, and no doubt they were an incentive to our thoughts as well as to those of the older girls, who went to "The Improvement Circle," and wrote compositions.

A year or two after this I attempted poetry, and my

verses began to appear in the newspapers, in one or two Annuals, and later in *The Lowell Offering.*

In 1846 I wrote some verses which were published in the *Lowell Journal,* and these caused me to make the acquaintance of the sub-editor of that paper, who afterwards became my life companion. I speak of this here because, in my early married life, I found the exact help that I needed for continued education,—the leisure to read good books, sent to my husband for review, in the quiet of my secluded home. For I had neither the gowns to wear nor the disposition to go into society, and as my companion was not willing to go without me, in the long evenings, when the children were in bed and I was busy making "auld claes look amaist as good as new," (old clothes look almost as good as new) he read aloud to me countless books on abstruse political and general subjects, which I never should have thought of reading for myself.

These are the "books that have helped me." In fact, of all the books I have read, I remember but very few that have not helped me. Thus I had the companionship of a mind more mature, wiser, and less prone to unrealities than my own; and if it seems to the reader that my story is that of one of the more fortunate ones among the working-girls of my time, it is because of this needed help, which I received almost at the beginning of my womanhood. And for this, as well as for those early days of poverty and toil, I am devoutly and reverently thankful.

The religious experience of a young person oftentimes forms a large part of the early education or development; and mine is peculiar, since I am one of the very few persons, in this country at least, who have been excommunicated from a Protestant church. And I cannot speak of this event without showing the strong sectarian tendencies of the time.

As late as 1843–1845 Puritan orthodoxy still held sway over nearly the whole of New England; and the gloomy doctrines of Jonathan Edwards, now called his "philosophy," held a mighty grasp on the minds of the people, all other denominations being frowned upon. The Episcopal church was considered "little better than the Catholic," and the Universalists and the Unitarians were treated with even less tolerance by the "Evangelicals" than any sect outside these denominations is treated today. The charge against the Unitarians was that they did not believe *all* of the Bible, and that they preached "mere morality rather than religion."

My mother, who had sat under the preaching of the Rev. Paul Dean, in Boston, had early drifted away from her hereditary church and its beliefs; but she had always sent her children to the Congregational church and Sunday-school, not wishing, perhaps, to run the same risk for their souls that she was willing to take for her own, thus keeping us on the "safe side," as it was called, with regard to our eternal salvation. Consequently, we were well taught in the belief of a literal devil, in a lake of brimstone and fire, and in the "wrath of a just God."

The terrors of an imaginative child's mind, into which these monstrous doctrines were poured, can hardly be described, and their lasting effect need not be dwelt upon. It was natural that young people who had minds of their own should be attracted to the new doctrine of a Father's love, as well as to the ministers who preached it; and thus in a short time the mill girls and boys made a large part of the congregation of those "unbelieving" sects which had come to disturb the "ancient solitary reign" of primitive New England orthodoxy.

I used often to wish that I could go to the Episcopal Sunday-school, because their little girls were not afraid of the devil, were allowed to dance, and had so much nicer books in their Sunday-school library. "Little Henry and his Bearer," and "The Lady of the Manor," in which was the story of "The Beautiful Estelle," were lent to me; and the last-named was a delight and an inspiration. But the little "orthodox" girls were not allowed to read even religious novels; and one of my work-mates, whose name would surprise the reader, and who afterwards outgrew such prejudices, took me to task for buying a paper copy of Scott's "Redgauntlet," saying, "Why, Hattie, do you not know that it is a *novel?*"

We had frequent discussions among ourselves on the different texts of the Bible, and debated such questions as, "Is it a sin to read novels?" "Is it right to read secular books on Sunday?" or, "Is it wicked to play cards or checkers?" By this it will be seen that we were made more familiar with the form, than with the spirit or the teaching, of Christianity.

In the spring of 1840 there was a great revival in Lowell, and some of the little girls held prayer-meetings, after school, at each other's houses, and many of them "experienced religion." I went sometimes to these meetings, and one night, when I was walking home by starlight, for the days were still short, one of the older girls said to me, "Are you happy?" "Do you love Jesus?" "Do you want to be saved?"—"Why, yes," I answered. "Then you have experienced religion," said the girl; "you are converted." I was startled at the idea, but did not know how to deny it, and I went home in an exalted state of feeling; and, as I looked into the depths of the heavens above me, there came to my youthful mind the first glimmer of thought on spiritual themes.

It was an awakening, but not a conversion, for I had been converted *from* nothing *to* nothing. I was at once claimed as a "young convert," went to the church prayer-meeting, told my "experience" as directed, and was put on probation for admission to the church. Meanwhile, I had been advised not to ask my mother's consent to this step, because she was a Universalist, and might object. But I did not follow this advice; and when I told her of my desire, she simply answered, "If you think it will make you any happier, do so, but I do not believe you will be satisfied." I have always been very thankful to my mother for giving me this freedom in my young life,—

"Not to be followed hourly, watched and noosed,"—

this chance in such an important matter to learn to think and to act for myself. In fact, she always carried out this principle, and never to my recollection coerced her children on any important point, but taught them to "see for themselves."

When the day came for me to be admitted into the church, I, with many other little girls, was sprinkled; and, when I stood up to repeat the creed, I can truly say that I knew no more what were the doctrines to which I was expected to subscribe, than I did about the Copernican System or the Differential Calculus. And I might have said, with the disciples at Ephesus, I "have not so much as heard whether there be any Holy Ghost." For, although I had been regularly to church and to Sunday-school, I had never seen the Articles of Belief, nor had I been instructed concerning the doctrines, or the sacredness of the vow I was about to take upon me. Nor, from the frequent backsliding among the young converts, do I think my case was a singular one, although, so far as I know, I was the only one who *backslid* enough to be excommunicated.

And later, when I was requested to subscribe to the Articles of Belief, I found I could not accept them, particularly a certain part, which related to the day of judgment and what would follow thereafter. I have reviewed this document, and am able to quote the exact words which were a stumbling-block to me. "We believe...that at the day of judgment the state of all will be unalterably fixed, and that the punishment of the wicked and the happiness of the righteous will be endless."

When the service was over, I went home, feeling as if I had done something wrong. I thought of my mother, whom my church people called an "unbeliever;" of my dear little brother who had been drowned, and whose soul might be LOST, and I was most unhappy. In fact, so serious was I for many days, that no doubt my church friends thought me a most promising young convert.

Indeed I was converted, but not in the way they supposed; for I had begun to think on religious subjects, and the more I thought the less I believed in the doctrines of the church to which I belonged. Doubts of the goodness of God filled my mind, and unbelief in the Father's love and compassion darkened my young life. What a conversion! The beginning of long years of doubt and of struggle in search of spiritual truths.

After a time I went no more to my church meetings, and began to attend those of the Universalists; but, though strongly urged, as a "come-outer," to join that body, I did not do so, being fearful of subscribing to a belief whose mysteries I could neither understand nor explain.

Hearing that I was attending the meetings of another denomination, my church appointed three persons, at least one of whom was a deacon, to labor with me. They came to our house one evening, and, while my mother and I sat at our sewing, they plied me with questions relating to my duty as a church member, and arguments concerning the articles of belief; these I did not know how to answer, but my mother, who had had some experience in "religious" disputes, gave text for text, and I remember that, although I trembled at her boldness, I thought she had the best of it.

Meanwhile, I sat silent, with downcast eyes, and when they threatened me with excommunication if I did not go to the church meetings, and "fulfil my covenant," I mustered up courage to say, with shaking voice, "I do not believe; I cannot go to your church, even if you do excommunicate me."

When my Universalist friends heard of this threat of excommunication, they urged the preparation of a letter to the church, giving my reasons for non-attendance; and this was published in a Lowell newspaper, July 30, 1842. In this letter, which my elder brother helped me to prepare,—in fact, I believe wrote the most of it,—several arguments against the Articles of Belief are given; and the letter closes with a request to "my brothers and sisters," to erase my name from "your church books rather than to follow your usual course, common in cases similar to my own, to excommunicate the heretic."

This request was not heeded, and shortly after a committee of three was "then appointed to take farther steps;" and this committee reported that they had "visited and admonished" me without success; and in November, 1842, the following vote was passed, and is recorded in the church book:—

"Nov. 21, 1842.

Whereas, it appears that Miss Harriet Hanson has violated her covenant with this church,—first, by repeated and regular absence from the ordinances of the gospel, second, by embracing sentiments deemed by this church heretical; and whereas, measures have been taken to reclaim her, but ineffectual; therefore,

Voted, that we withdraw our fellowship from the said Miss Hanson until she shall give satisfactory evidence of repentance."

And thus, at seventeen years of age, I was excommunicated from the church of my ancestors, and for no fault, no sin, no crime, but simply because I could not subscribe conscientiously to doctrines which I did not comprehend. I relate this phase of my youthful experience here in detail, because it serves to show the methods which were then in use to cast out or dispose of those members who could not subscribe to the doctrines of the dominant church of New England.

For some time after this, I was quite in disgrace with some of my work-mates, and was called a "heretic" and a "child of perdition" by my church friends. But, as I did not agree, even in this, with their opinions, but went my "ain gait," it followed that, although I remained for a time something of a heretic, I was not an unbeliever in sacred things nor did I prove to be a "child of perdition." But this experience made me very unhappy, and gave me a distate for religious reading and thinking, and for many years the Bible was a sealed book to me, until I came to see in the Book, not the letter of dogma, but rather the spirit of truth and of revelation. This experience also repressed the humorous side of my nature, which is every one's birthright, and made me for a time a sort of youthful cynic; and I allowed myself to feel a certain contempt for those of my work-mates who, though they could not give clear reason for their belief, still remained faithful to their "covenant."

There were two or three little incidents connected with this episode in my life that may be of interest. A little later, when I thought of applying for the position of teaching in a public school, I was advised by a well-meaning friend not to attempt it, "for," the friend added, "you will not succeed, for how can a Universalist *pray* in her school?"

Several years after my excommunication, when I had come to observe that religion and "mere morality" do not always go together, I had a final interview with one of the deacons who had labored with me. He was an overseer in the room where I worked, and I had noticed his familiar manner with some of the girls, who did not like it any better than I did; and one day, when his behavior was unusually offensive, I determined to speak to him about it.

I called him to my drawing-in frame, where I was sitting at work, and said to him something like this: "I have hard work to believe that *you* are one of those deacons who came to labor with a young girl about belonging to your church. I don't think you set the example of good works you then preached to me." He gave me a look, but did not answer; and shortly after, as I might have expected, I received an "honorable discharge" from his room.

But let me acknowledge one far-reaching benefit that resulted from my being admitted to the Orthodox church, a benefit which came to me in the summer of 1895. Because of my baptism, administered so long ago, I was enabled to officiate as god-mother to my grandchild and namesake, in Pueblo, Colorado,—one among the first of the little girls born on a political equality with the little boys of that enlightened State, born, as one may say, with the ballot in her hand! And to any reader who has an interest in the final result of my religious experience, I may add, that, as late as 1898, I became a communicant of the Episcopal Church.

When the time came for me to become engaged to the man of my choice, having always believed in the old-fashioned idea that there should be no secrets between persons about to marry, I told him, among my other shortcomings, as the most serious of all, the story of my excommunication. To my great surprise, he laughed heartily, derided the whole affair, and wondered at the serious view I had always taken of it; and later he enjoyed saying to some of his gentlemen friends, as if it were a good joke, "Did you know my wife had been excommunicated from the church?"

And I too, long since have learned, that no creed—

"Can fix our doom,
Nor stay the eternal Love from His intent,
While Hope remaining bears her verdant bloom."

CHAPTER IV.

THE CHARACTERISTICS OF THE EARLY
FACTORY GIRLS.

WHEN I look back into the factory life of fifty or sixty years ago, I do not see what is called "a class" of young men and women going to and from their daily work, like so many ants that cannot be distinguished one from another; I see them as individuals, with personalities of their own. This one has about her the atmosphere of her early home. That one is impelled by a strong and noble purpose. The other,—what she is, has been an influence for good to me and to all womankind.

Yet they were a class of factory operatives, and were spoken of (as the same class is spoken of now) as a set of persons who earned their daily bread, whose condition was fixed, and who must continue to spin and to weave to the end of their natural existence. Nothing but this was expected of them, and they were not supposed to be capable of social or mental improvement. That they could be educated and developed into something more than mere work-people, was an idea that had not yet entered the public mind. So little does one class of persons really know about the thoughts and aspirations of another! It was the good fortune of these early mill-girls to teach the people of that time that this sort of labor is not degrading; that the operative is not only "capable of virtue," but also capable of self-cultivation.

At the time the Lowell cotton-mills were started, the factory girl was the lowest among women. In England, and in France particularly, great injustice had been done to her real character; she was represented as subjected to influences that could not fail to destroy her purity and self-respect. In the eyes of her overseer she was but a brute, a slave, to be beaten, pinched, and pushed about.

It was to overcome this prejudice that such high wages
had been offered to women that they might be induced
to become mill-girls, in spite of the opprobrium that still
clung to this "degrading occupation." At first only a few
came; for, though tempted by the high wages to be regularly paid in "cash," there were many who still preferred
to go on working at some more *genteel* employment at
seventy-five cents a week and their board.

But in a short time the prejudice against factory labor
wore away, and the Lowell mills became filled with bloom-
ing and energetic New England women. They were naturally intelligent, had mother-wit, and fell easily into the
ways of their new life. They soon began to associate with
those who formed the community in which they had come
to live, and were invited to their houses. They went to
the same church, and sometimes married into some of
the best families. Or if they returned to their secluded
homes again, instead of being looked down upon as "factory girls" by the squire's or the lawyer's family, they
were more often welcomed as coming from the metropolis,
bringing new fashions, new books, and new ideas with
them.

In 1831 Lowell was little more than a factory village.
Several corporations were started, and the cotton-mills
belonging to them were building. Help was in great demand; and stories were told all over the country of the
new factory town, and the high wages that were offered
to all classes of work-people,—stories that reached the
ears of mechanics' and farmers' sons, and gave new life
to lonely and dependent women in distant towns and
farmhouses. Into this Yankee El Dorado, these needy people began to pour by the various modes of travel known
to those slow old days. The stage-coach and the canal-
boat came every day, always filled with new recruits
for this army of useful people. The mechanic and machinist
came, each with his home-made chest of tools, and oftentimes his wife and little ones. The widow came with her
little flock and her scanty housekeeping goods to open
a boarding-house or variety store, and so provided a home
for her fatherless children. Many farmers' daughters came

to earn money to complete their wedding outfit, or buy the bride's share of housekeeping articles.

Women with past histories came, to hide their griefs and their identity, and to earn an honest living in the "sweat of their brow." Single young men came, full of hope and life, to get money for an education, or to lift the mortgage from the home-farm. Troops of young girls came by stages and baggage-wagons, men often being employed to go to other States and to Canada, to collect them at so much a head, and deliver them at the factories.

A very curious sight these country girls presented to young eyes accustomed to a more modern style of things. When the large covered baggage-wagon arrived in front of a block on the corporation, they would descend from it, dressed in various and outlandish fashions, and with their arms brimful of bandboxes containing all their worldly goods. On each of these was sewed a card, on which one could read the old-fashioned New England name of the owner. And sorrowful enough they looked, even to the fun-loving child who has lived to tell the story; for they had all left their pleasant country homes to try their fortunes in a great manufacturing town, and they were homesick even before they landed at the doors of their boarding-houses. Years after, this scene dwelt in my memory; and whenever anyone said anything about being homesick, there rose before me the picture of a young girl with a sorrowful face and a big tear in each eye, clambering down the steps at the rear of a great covered wagon, holding fast to a cloth-covered bandbox, drawn up at the top with a string, on which was sewed a paper bearing the name of Plumy Clay!

Some of these girls brought diminutive hair trunks covered with the skin of calves, spotted in dun and white, even as when they did skip and play in daisy-blooming meads. And when several of them were set together in front of one of the blocks, they looked like their living counterparts, reposing at noontide in the adjacent field. One of this kind of trunks has been handed down to me as an heirloom. The hair is worn off in patches; it cannot

be invigorated, and it is now become a hairless heirloom. Within its hide-bound sides are safely stowed
away the love-letters of a past generation,—love-letters
that agitated the hearts of the grandparents of to-day;
and I wonder that their resistless ardor has not long
ago burst its wrinkled sides. It is relegated to distant at-
tics, with its ancient crony, "ye bandbox," to enjoy an
honored and well-earned repose.

Ah me! when some of us, its contemporaries, are also
past our usefulness, gone clean out of fashion, may we
also be as resigned, yea, as willing, to be laid quietly on
some attic shelf!

These country girls had queer names, which added to
the singularity of their appearance. Samantha, Triphena,
Plumy, Kezia, Aseneth, Elgardy, Leafy, Ruhamah, Lovey,
Almaretta, Sarepta, and Florilla were among them.

Their dialect was also very peculiar. On the broken
English and Scotch of their ancestors was ingrafted the
nasal Yankee twang; so that many of them, when they
had just come *daown,* spoke a language almost unintelli-
gible. But the severe discipline and ridicule which met
them was as good as a school education, and they were
soon taught the "city way of speaking."

Their dress was also peculiar, and was of the plainest
of homespun, cut in such an old-fashioned style that each
young girl looked as if she had borrowed her grandmother's gown. Their only head-covering was a shawl, which
was pinned under the chin; but after the first payday, a
"shaker" (or "scooter") sunbonnet usually replaced this
primitive head-gear of their rural life.

But the early factory girls were not all country girls.
There were others also, who had been taught that "work
is no disgrace." There were some who came to Lowell
solely on account of the social or literary advantages
to be found there. They lived in secluded parts of New
England, where books were scarce, and there was no
cultivated society. They had comfortable homes, and did
not perhaps need the *money* they would earn; but they
longed to see this new "City of Spindles," of which they
had heard so much from their neighbors and friends, who

had gone there to work.

And the fame of the circulating libraries, that were soon opened, drew them and kept them there, when no other inducement would have been sufficient.

The laws relating to women were such, that a husband could claim his wife wherever he found her, and also the children she was trying to shield from his influence; and I have seen more than one poor woman skulk behind her loom or her frame when visitors were approaching the end of the aisle where she worked. Some of these were known under assumed names, to prevent their husbands from trusteeing their wages. It was a very common thing for a male person of a certain kind to do this, thus depriving his wife of *all* her wages, perhaps, month after month. The wages of minor children could be trusteed, unless the children (being fourteen years of age) were given their time. Women's wages were also trusteed for the debts of their husbands, and children's for the debts of their parents.

As an instance, my mother had some financial difficulties when I was fifteen years old, and to save herself and me from annoyance, she gave me my time. The document reads as follows:—

"Be it known that I, Harriet Hanson, of Lowell, in consideration that my minor daughter Harriet J. has taken upon herself the whole burden of her own support, and has undertaken and agreed to maintain herself henceforward without expense to me, do hereby release and quitclaim unto her all profits and wages which she may hereafter earn or acquire by her skill or labor in any occupation,—and do hereby disclaim all right to collect or interfere with the same. And I do give and release unto her the absolute control and disposal of her own time according to her own discretion, without interference from me. It being understood that I am not to be chargeable hereafter with any expense on her account.

(Signed) HARRIET HANSON.

July 2, 1840."

It must be remembered that at this date woman had no property rights. A widow could be left without her share of her husband's (or the family) property, a legal "incumbrance" to his estate. A father could make his will without reference to his daughter's share of the inheritance. He usually left her a home on the farm as long as she remained single. A woman was not supposed to be capable of spending her own or of using other people's money. In Massachusetts, before 1840, a woman could not legally be treasurer of her own sewing-society, unless some man were responsible for her.

The law took no cognizance of woman as a money-spender. She was a ward, an appendage, a relict. Thus it happened, that if a woman did not choose to marry, or, when left a widow, to re-marry, she had no choice but to enter one of the few employments open to her, or to become a burden on the charity of some relative.

In almost every New England home could be found one or more of these women, sometimes welcome, more often unwelcome, and leading joyless, and in many instances unsatisfactory, lives. The cotton-factory was a great opening to these lonely and dependent women. From a condition approaching pauperism they were at once placed above want; they could earn money, and spend it as they pleased; and could gratify their tastes and desires without restraint, and without rendering an account to anybody. At last they had found a place in the universe; they were no longer obliged to finish out their faded lives mere burdens to male relatives. Even the *time* of these women was their own, on Sundays and in the evening after the day's work was done. For the first time in this country woman's labor had a money value. She had become not only an earner and a producer, but also a spender of money, a recognized factor in the political economy of her time. And thus a long upward step in our material civilization was taken; woman had begun to earn and hold her own money, and through its aid had learned to think and to act for herself.

Among the older women who sought this new employment were very many lonely and dependent ones, such as used to be mentioned in old wills as "incumbrances" and "relicts," and to whom a chance of earning money was indeed a new revelation. How well I remember some of these solitary ones! As a child of eleven years, I often made fun of them—for children do not see the pathetic side of human life—and imitated their limp carriage and inelastic gait. I can see them now, even after sixty years, just as they looked,—depressed, modest, mincing, hardly daring to look one in the face, so shy and sylvan had been their lives. But after the first pay-day came, and they felt the jingle of silver in their pockets, and had begun to feel its mercurial influence, their bowed heads were lifted, their necks seemed braced with steel, they looked you in the face, sang blithely among their looms or frames, and walked with elastic step to and from their work. And when Sunday came, homespun was no longer their only wear; and how sedately gay in their new attire they walked to church, and how proudly they dropped their silver four-pences into the contribution-box! It seemed as if a great hope impelled them,—the harbinger of the new era that was about to dawn for them and for all women-kind.

In passing, let me not forget to pay a tribute, also, to those noble single and widowed women, who are "set solitary in families," but whose presence cements the domestic fabric, and whose influence is unseen and oftentimes unappreciated, until they are taken away and the integral part of the old home-life begins to crumble.

Except in rare instances, the rights of the early mill-girls were secure. They were subject to no extortion, if they did extra work they were always paid in full, and their own account of labor done by the piece was always accepted. They kept the figures, and were paid accordingly. This was notably the case with the weavers and drawing-in girls. Though the hours of labor were long, they were not overworked; they were obliged to tend no more looms and frames than they could easily take care of, and they had plenty of time to sit and rest. I have known a girl to sit idle twenty or thirty minutes at a time. They were not driven, and their work-a-day life was made easy. They were treated with consideration by their employers, and there was a feeling of respectful equality between them. The most

favored of the girls were sometimes invited to the houses
of the dignitaries of the mills, showing that the line of
social division was not rigidly maintained.

Their life in the factory was made pleasant to them. In
those days there was no need of advocating the doctrine of
the proper relation between employer and employed. *Help
was too valuable to be ill-treated.* If these early agents, or
overseers, had been disposed to exercise undue authority,
or to establish unjust or arbitrary laws, the high character
of the operatives, and the fact that women employees were
scarce would have prevented it. A certain agent of one of
the first corporations in Lowell (an old sea-captain) said
to one of his boarding-house keepers, "I should like to
rule my help as I used to rule my sailors, but so many of
them are women I do not dare to do it."

The knowledge of the antecedents of these operatives
was the safeguard of their liberties. The majority of them
were as well born as their "overlookers," if not better;
and they were also far better educated.

The agents and overseers were usually married men,
with families of growing sons and daughters. They were
members, and sometimes deacons, of the church, and
teachers in the same Sunday-school with the girls employed
under them. They were generally of good morals and tem-
perate habits, and often exercised a good influence over
their help. The feeling that the agents and overseers were
interested in their welfare caused the girls, in turn, to feel
an interest in the work for which their employers were responsible. The conscientious among them took as much
pride in spinning a smooth thread, drawing in a perfect
web, or in making good cloth, as they would have done if
the material had been for their own wearing. And thus
was practised, long before it was preached, that principle
of true political economy,—the just relation, the mutual
interest, that ought to exist between employers and employed.

Those of the mill-girls who had homes generally worked
from eight to ten months in the year; the rest of the time
was spent with parents or friends. A few taught school dur-

ing the summer months.

When we left the mill, or changed our place of work from one corporation to another, we were given an "honorable discharge." Mine, of which I am still quite proud, is dated the year of my marriage, and is as follows:—

"HARRIET J. HANSON has been employed in the Boott Cotton Mills, in a dressing-room, twenty-five months, and is honorably discharged."

(Signed) J. F. TROTT.

LOWELL, *July* 25, 1848."

The chief characteristics of the early mill-girls may be briefly mentioned, as showing the material of which this new community of working-women was composed. Concerning their personal appearance, I am able to quote from a magazine article written by the poet John G. Whittier, then a resident of Lowell. He thus describes,—

"THE FACTORY GIRLS OF LOWELL.

"Acres of girlhood, beauty reckoned by the square rod,—or miles by long measure! the young, the graceful, the gay,—the flowers gathered from a thousand hillsides and green valleys of New England, fair unveiled Nuns of Industry, Sisters of Thrift, and are ye not also Sisters of Charity dispensing comfort and hope and happiness around many a hearthstone of your native hills, making sad faces cheerful, and hallowing age and poverty with the sunshine of your youth and love! Who shall sneer at your calling? Who shall count your vocation otherwise than noble and ennobling?"

Of their literary and studious habits, Professor A. P. Peabody, of Harvard University, gives his opinion in an article written not long ago in the *Atlantic Monthly*. He says, "During the palmy days of *The Lowell Offering* I used every winter to lecture for the Lowell Lyceum. Not amusement, but instruction, was then the lecturer's aim.... The Lowell Hall was always crowded, and four-fifths of the audience were factory-girls. When the lecturer entered, almost every girl had a book in her hand, and was intent upon it. When he rose, the book was laid aside, and paper and pencil taken instead; and there were very few who did not carry home full notes of what they had heard. I have never seen anywhere so assiduous note-taking. No, not even in a college class,... as in that assembly of young women, laboring for their subsistence."

To introduce a more practical side of their character I will quote an extract from a letter received not long ago from a gentleman in the Detroit Public Library, which says, "The factory-girls went to Lowell from the hills of Vermont when I was a boy, numbers of them from every town in my county (Windsor); and it was considered something of a distinction to have worked for 'the corporation,' and brought home some hard cash, which in many and many cases went to help lift a mortgage on the farm, or to buy something needed for the comfort of the old folks, or to send a younger brother or sister to the Academy. I knew several of these girls who brought home purses from Lowell which looked big in those days, and I recall one who is still living in my native town of Pomfret."

It may be added here, that the majority of the mill-girls made just as good use of their money, so newly earned, and of whose value they had hitherto known so little. They were necessarily industrious. They were also frugal and saving. It was their custom on the first day of every month, after paying their board-bill ($1.25 a week), to put their wages in the savings-bank. There the money stayed, on interest, until they withdrew it, to carry home or to use for a special purpose. It is easy to see how much good this sum would do in a rural community where money, as a means of exchange, had been scarce. Into the barren homes many of them had left it went like a quiet stream, carrying with it beauty and refreshment. The mortgage was lifted from the homestead; the farmhouse was painted; the barn rebuilt; modern improvements (including Mrs. Child's "Frugal Housewife"—the first American cook-book) were introduced into the mother's kitchen, and books and newspapers began to ornament the sitting-room table.

Some of the mill-girls helped maintain widowed mothers, or drunken, incompetent, or invalid fathers. Many of them educated the younger children of the family, and young men were sent to college with the money furnished by the untiring industry of their women relatives.

Indeed, the most prevailing incentive to our labor was to secure the means of education for some *male* member of the family. To make a *gentleman* of a brother or a son, to give him a college education, was the dominant thought in the minds of a great many of these provident mill-girls. I have known more than one to give every cent of her wages, month after month, to her brother, that he might get the education necessary to enter some profession. I have known a mother to work years in this way for her boy. I have known women to educate by their earnings young men who were not sons or relatives. There are men now living who were helped to an education by the wages of the early mill-girls.

In speaking of this subject, Mr. Thomas Wentworth Higginson says,—

"I think it was the late President Walker who told me that in his judgment one-quarter of the men in Harvard College were being carried through by the special self-denial and sacrifices of women. I cannot answer for the ratio; but I can testify to having been an instance of this myself, and to having known a never-ending series of such cases of self-devotion."

Lowell, in this respect, was indeed a remarkable town, and it might be said of it, as of Thrums in "Auld Licht Idyls," "There are scores and scores of houses in it that have sent their sons to college (by what a struggle), some to make their way to the front in their professions, and others, perhaps, despite their broadcloth, never to be a patch upon their parents."

The early mill-girls were religious by nature and by Puritan inheritance, true daughters of those men and women who, as some one has said, "were as devoted to education as they were to religion;" for they planted the church and the schoolhouse side by side. On entering the mill, each one was obliged to sign a "regulation paper" which required her to attend regularly some place of public worship. They were of many denominations. In one boarding-house that I knew, there were girls belonging to eight different religious sects.

In 1843, there were in Lowell fourteen regularly organized religious societies. Ten of these constituted a "Sabbath School Union," which consisted of over five thousand scholars and teachers; three-fourths of the scholars, and a large proportion of the teachers, were mill-girls. Once a year, every Fourth of July, this "Sabbath School Union," each section, or division, under its own sectarian banner, marched in procession to the grove on Chapel Hill, where a picnic was held, with lemonade, and long speeches by the ministers of the different churches,—speeches which the little boys and girls did not seem to think were made to be listened to.

The mill-girls went regularly to meeting and "Sabbath-school;" and every Sunday the streets of Lowell were alive with neatly dressed young women, going or returning therefrom. Their fine appearance on "the Sabbath" was often spoken of by strangers visiting Lowell.

Dr. Scoresby, in his "American Factories and their Operatives," (with selections from *The Lowell Offering,*) holds up the Lowell mill-girls to their sister operatives of Bradford, England, as an example of neatness and good behavior. Indeed, it was a pretty sight to see so many wide-awake young girls in the bloom of life, clad in their holiday dresses,—

"Whose delicate feet to the Temple of God,
   Seemed to move as if wings had carried them there."

The morals of these girls were uniformly good. The regulation paper, before spoken of, required each one to be of good moral character; and if any one proved to be disreputable, she was very soon turned out of the mill. Their standard of behavior was high, and the majority kept aloof from those who were suspected of wrong-doing. They had, perhaps, less temptation than the working-girls of to-day, since they were not required to dress beyond their means, and comfortable homes were provided by their employers, where they could board cheaply. Their surroundings were pure, and the whole atmosphere of their boarding-houses was as refined as that of their own homes. They expected men to treat them with courtesy; they looked forward to becoming the wives of good men. Their attitude was that of the German *Fraulein,* who said, "Treat every maiden with respect, for you do not know whose *wife* she will be."

But there were exceptions to the general rule,—just enough to prove the doctrine of averages; there were girls who came to the mill to work whom no one knew anything about, but they did not stay long, the life there being "too clean for them."

The health of the girls was good. The regularity and simplicity of their lives, and the plain and substantial food provided for them, kept them free from illness. From their Puritan ancestry they had inherited sound bodies and a fair share of endurance. Fevers and similar diseases were rare among them; they had no time to pet small ailments; the boarding-house mother was often both nurse and doctor, and so the physician's fee was saved. It may be said that, at that time, there was but one *pathy* and no "faith cures" nor any "science" to be supported by the many diseases "that flesh is heir to."

By reading the weekly newspapers the girls became interested in public events; they knew all about the Mexican war, and the anti-slavery cause had its adherents among them. Lectures on the doctrine of Fourier were read, or listened to, but none of them were "carried away" with the idea of spending their lives in large "phalansteries," as they seemed too much like cotton-factories to be models for their own future housekeeping.

The Brook Farm experiment was familiar to some of them; but the fault of this scheme was apparent to the practical ones who foresaw that a few would have to do all the manual labor and that an undue share would naturally fall to those who had already contracted the working-habit.

Mrs. Amelia Bloomer, one of the early pioneers of the dress-reform movement, found followers in Lowell; and parlor meetings were held at some of the boarding-houses to discuss the feasibility of this great revolution in the style of woman's dress. *The Lowell Journal* of 1850 states that on the Fourth of July a party of "Bloomerites" walked in the procession through the public streets, and *The London Punch* embellished its pages with a neat cartoon, a fashion-plate showing the different styles of the Bloomer costume. This first attempt at a reform in woman's dress was ridiculed out of existence by "public opinion;" but from it has been evolved the modern bicycle costume, now worn by women cyclers.

It seems to have been the fashion of the mill-girls to appear in procession on all public occasions. Mr. Cowley, in his "History of Lowell," speaks of President Jackson's visit to that city in 1833. He says: "On the day the President came, all the lady operatives turned out to meet him. They walked in procession, like troops of liveried angels clothed in white [with green-fringed parasols], with cannons booming, drums beating, banners flying, handkerchiefs waving, etc. The old hero was not more moved by the bullets that whistled round him in the battle of New Orleans than by the exhilarating spectacle here presented, and remarked, 'They are very pretty women, by the Eternal!' "

CHAPTER V.

CHARACTERISTICS (CONTINUED).

ONE of the first strikes of cotton-factory operatives that ever took place in this country was that in Lowell, in October, 1836. When it was announced that the wages were to be cut down, great indignation was felt, and it was decided to strike, *en masse.* This was done. The mills were shut down, and the girls went in procession from their several corporations to the "grove" on Chapel Hill, and listened to "incendiary" speeches from early labor reformers.

One of the girls stood on a pump, and gave vent to the feelings of her companions in a neat speech, declaring that it was their duty to resist all attempts at cutting down the wages. This was the first time a woman had spoken in public in Lowell, and the event caused surprise and consternation among her audience.

Cutting down the wages was not their only grievance, nor the only cause of this strike. Hitherto the corporations had paid twenty-five cents a week towards the board of each operative, and now it was their purpose to have the girls pay the sum; and this, in addition to the cut in wages, would make a difference of at least one dollar a week. It was estimated that as many as twelve or fifteen hundred girls turned out, and walked in procession through the streets. They had neither flags nor music, but sang songs, a favorite (but rather inappropriate) one being a parody on "I won't be a nun."

> "Oh! isn't it a pity, such a pretty girl as I—
> Should be sent to the factory to pine away and die?
> Oh! I cannot be a slave,
> I will not be a slave,
> For I'm so fond of liberty
> That I cannot be a slave."

My own recollection of this first strike (or "turn out" as it was called) is very vivid. I worked in a lower room, where I had heard the proposed strike fully, if not vehemently, discussed; I had been an ardent listener to what was said against this attempt at "oppression" on the part of the corporation, and naturally I took sides with the strikers. When the day came on which the girls were to turn out, those in the upper rooms started first, and so many of them left that our mill was at once shut down. Then, when the girls in my room stood irresolute, uncertain what to do, asking each other, "Would you?" or "Shall we turn out?" and not one of them having the courage to lead off, I, who began to think they would not go out, after all their talk, became impatient, and started on ahead, saying, with childish bravado, "I don't care what you do, *I* am going to turn out, whether any one else does or not;" and I marched out, and was followed by the others.[1]

As I looked back at the long line that followed me, I was more proud than I have ever been since at any success I may have achieved, and more proud than I shall ever be again until my own beloved State gives to its women citizens the right of suffrage.

The agent of the corporation where I then worked took some small revenges on the supposed ringleaders; on the principle of sending the weaker to the wall, my mother was turned away from her boarding-house, that functionary saying, "Mrs. Hanson, you could not prevent the older girls from turning out, but your daughter is a child, and *her* you could control."

It is hardly necessary to say that so far as results were concerned this strike did no good. The dissatisfaction of the operatives subsided, or burned itself out, and though the authorities did not accede to their demands, the majority returned to their work, and the corporation went on cutting down the wages.

And after a time, as the wages became more and more reduced, the best portion of the girls left and went to their

---

[1] I was then eleven years and eight months old. H.H.R.

homes, or to the other employments that were fast opening to women, until there were very few of the old guard left; and thus the *status* of the factory population of New England gradually became what we know it to be to-day.

Some of us took part in a political campaign, for the first time, in 1840, when William H. Harrison, the first Whig President, was elected; we went to the political meetings, sat in the gallery, heard speeches against Van Buren and the Democratic party, and helped sing the great campaign song beginning:—

"Oh have you heard the news of late?"

the refrain of which was:

"Tippecanoe and Tyler too,
Oh with them we'll beat little Van, Van,
Van is a used-up man."

And we named our sunbonnets "log-cabins," and set our teacups (we drank from saucers then) in little glass tea-plates, with log-cabins impressed on the bottom. The part the Lowell mill-girls took in these and similar events serves to show how wide-awake and up to date many of these middle-century working-women were.

Among the *fads* of those days may be mentioned those of the "water-cure" and the "Grahamite." The former was a theory of doctoring by means of cold water, used as packs, daily baths, and immoderate drinks. Quite a number of us adopted this practice, and one at least has not even yet wholly abandoned it.

Several members of my mother's family adopted "Professor" Graham's regimen, and for a few months we ate no meat, nor, as he said, "anything that had life in it." It was claimed that this would regenerate the race; that by following a certain line of diet, a person would live longer, do better work, and be able to endure any hardship, in fact, that not what we were, but what we ate, would be the making of us. Two young men, whom I knew, made their boasts that they had "walked from Boston to Lowell on an apple."

We ate fruit, vegetables, and unleavened or whole-wheat bread, baked in little round pats ("bullets," my mother called them), and without butter; there were no *relishes*. I soon got tired of the feeling of "goneness" this diet gave me; I found that although I might eat a pint of mashed potato, and the same quantity of squash, it was if I had not dined, and I gave up the experiment. But my elder brother, who had carried to the extremest extreme this "potato gospel," as Carlyle called it, induced my mother to make his Thanksgiving squash-pie after a receipt of his own. The crust was made of Indian meal and water, and the filling was of squash, water, and sugar! And he ate it, and called it good. But I thought then, and still think, that his enjoyment of the eating was in the principle rather than in the pie.

A few of the girls were interested in phrenology; and we had our heads examined by Professor Fowler, who, if not the first, was the chief exponent of this theory in Lowell. He went about into all the schools, examining children's heads. Mine, he said, "lacked veneration;" and this I supposed was an awful thing, because my teacher looked so reproachfully at me when the professor said it.

A few were interested in Mesmerism; and those of us who had the power to make ourselves *en rapport* with others tried experiments on "subjects," and sometimes held meetings in the evening for that purpose.

The life in the boarding-houses was very agreeable. These houses belonged to the corporation, and were usually kept by widows (mothers of mill-girls), who were often the friends and advisers of their boarders.

Among these may be mentioned the mothers of Lucy Larcom; the Hon. Gustavus Vasa Fox, once Assistant Secretary of the Navy; John W. Hanson, D.D.; the Rev. W. H. Cudworth; Major General B. F. Butler; and several others.

Each house was a village or community of itself. There fifty or sixty young women from different parts of New England met and lived together. When not at their work, by natural selection they sat in groups in their chambers, or in a corner of the large dining-room, busy at some agreeable employment; or they wrote letters, read, studied, or sewed, for, as a rule, they were their own seamstresses and dressmakers.

It is refreshing to remember their simplicity of dress; they wore no ruffles and very few ornaments. It is true that some of them had gold watches and gold pencils, but they were worn only on grand occasions; as a rule, the early mill-girls were not of that class that is said to be "always suffering for a breast-pin." Though their dress was so simple and so plain, yet it was so tasteful that they were often accused of looking like ladies; the complaint was sometimes made that no one could tell the difference in *church* between the factory-girls and the daughters of some of the first families in the city.

Mrs. Sarah J. Hale, in *The Lady's Book,* in 1842, speaking of the impossibility of considering dress a mark of distinction, says: "Many of the factory-girls wear gold watches and an imitation at least of all the ornaments which grace the daughters of our most opulent citizens."

The boarding-houses were considered so attractive that strangers, by invitation, often came to look in upon them, and see for themselves how the mill-girls lived. Dickens, in his "American Notes," speaks with surprise of their home life. He says, "There is a piano in a great many of the boarding-houses, and nearly all the young ladies subscribe to circulating libraries." There was a feeling of *esprit de corps* among these households; any advantage secured to one of the number was usually shared by others belonging to her set or group. Books were exchanged, letters from home were read, and "pieces," intended for the Improvement Circle, were presented for friendly criticism.

There was always a best room in the boarding-house, to entertain callers in; but if any of the girls had a regular gentleman caller, a special evening was set apart each week to receive him. This room was furnished with a carpet, sometimes with a piano, as Dickens says, and with the best furniture, including oftentimes the relics of household treasures left of the old-time gentility of the housemother.

This mutual acquaintanceship was of great advantage. They discussed the books they read, debated religious and social questions, compared their thoughts and experiences, and advised and helped one another. And so their mental growth went on, and they soon became educated far beyond what their mothers or their grandmothers could have been. The girls also stood by one another in the mills; when one wanted to be absent half a day, two or three others would tend an extra loom or frame apiece, so that the absent one might not lose her pay. At this time the mule and spinning-jenny had not been introduced; two or three looms, or spinning-frames, were as much as one girl was required to tend, more than that being considered "double work."

The inmates of what may be called these literary households were omniverous readers of books, and were also subscribers to the few magazines and literary newspapers; and it was their habit, after reading their copies, to send them by mail or stage-coach to their widely scattered homes, where they were read all over a village or a neighborhood; and thus was current literature introduced into by and lonely places.

From an article in *The Lowell Offering,* ("Our Household," signed H.T.,) I am able to quote a sketch of one factory boarding-house interior. The author said, "In our house there are eleven boarders, and in all thirteen members of the family. I will class them according to their religious tenets as follows: Calvinist Baptist, Unitarian, Congregational, Catholic, Episcopalian, and Mormonite, one each; Universalist and Methodist, two each; Christian Baptist, three. Their reading is from the following sources: They receive regularly fifteen newspapers and periodicals; these are, the *Boston Daily Times,* the *Herald of Freedom,* the *Signs of the Times,* and the *Christian Herald,* two copies each; the *Christian Register, Vox Populi, Literary Souvenir, Boston Pilot, Young Catholic's Friend, Star of Bethelehem,* and *The Lowell Offering,* three copies each. A magazine, one copy. We also borrow regularly the *Non-Resistant,* the *Liberator,* the *Lady's Book,* the *Ladies' Pearl,* and the *Ladies' Companion.* We have also in the house what perhaps cannot be found anywhere else in the city of Lowell,—a Mormon Bible."

The "magazine" mentioned may have been *The Dial,* that exponent of New England Transcendentalism, of which *The Offering* was the humble contemporary. The writer adds to her article: "Notwithstanding the divers faiths embraced among us, we live in much harmony, and seldom is difference of opinion the cause of dissensions among us." Novels were not very popular with us, as we inclined more to historical writings and to poetry. But such books as "Charlotte Temple," "Eliza Wharton," "Maria Monk," "The Arabian Nights," "The Mysteries of Udolpho," "Abellino, the Bravo of Venice," or "The Castle of Otranto," were sometimes taken from the circulating library, read with delight, and secretly lent from one young girl to another.

Our religious reading was confined to the Bible, Baxter's "Saints' Rest," "The Pilgrim's Progress," "The Religious Courtship," "The Widow Directed," and Sunday-school books.

It was fortunate for us that we were obliged to read good books, such as histories, the English classics, and the very few American novels that were then in existence. Cheap editions of Scott were but just publishing; "Pickwick," in serial numbers, soon followed; Frederika Bremer was hardly translated; Lydia Maria Child was beginning to write; Harriet Beecher Stowe was busy in her nursery, and the great American novel was not written,—nor yet the small one, which was indeed a blessing!

There were many representative women among us who did not voice their thoughts in writing, and whose names are not on the list of the contributers to *The Offering.* This was but one phase of their development, as many of them have exerted a widespread influence in other directions. They graduated from the cotton-factory, carrying with them the results of their manual training; and they have done their little part towards performing the useful labor of life. Into whatever vocation they entered they made practical use of the habits of industry and perseverance learned during those early years, and they have exemplified them in their stirring and fruitful lives.

In order to show how far the influence of individual effort may extend, it will be well to mention the after-fate of some of them. One became an artist of note, another a poet of more than local fame, a third an inventor, and several were among the pioneers in Florida, in Kansas, and in other Western States. A limited number married those who were afterwards doctors of divinity, major-generals, and members of Congress; and these, in more than one instance, had been their work-mates in the factory.

And in later years, when, through the death of the bread-winner, the pecuniary support of those dependent on him fell to their lot, some of these factory-girls carried on business, entered the trades, or went to college and thereby were enabled to practise in some of the professions. They thus resumed their old-time habit of supporting the helpless ones, and educating the children of the family.

These women were all self-made in the truest sense; and it is well to mention their success in life, that others, who now earn their living at what is called "ungenteel" employments, may see that what one does is not of so much importance as what one is. I do not know why it should not be just as commendable for a woman who has risen to have been once a factory-girl, as it is for an ex-governor or a major-general to have been a "bobbin-boy." A woman ought to be as proud of being self-made as a man; not proud in a boasting way, but proud enough to assert the fact in her life and in her works.

All these of whom I speak are widely scattered. I hear of them in the far West, in the South, and in foreign countries, even so far away as the Himalaya Mountains. But wherever they may be, I know that they will join with me in saying that the discipline of their youth helped to make them what they are; and that the cotton-factory was to them the means of education, their preparatory school, in which they learned the alphabet of their life-work.

Such is the brief story of the life of every-day working-girls; such as it was then, so it might be to-day. Undoubtedly there might have been another side to this picture, but I give the side I knew best,—the bright side!

CHAPTER VI.

THE LOWELL OFFERING AND ITS WRITERS.

One of the most curious phases in the life of New England, and one that must always puzzle the historian of its literature, is its sudden intellectual blossoming half a century ago.

Emerson says, "The children of New England between 1820 and 1840 were born with knives in their brains;" and this would seem to be true, since during or very near that time, were born the majority of those writers and thinkers whose lives have been so recently and so nobly rounded out,—Emerson, Bryant, Longfellow, Lowell, Whittier, John Pierpont,—they whose influence cannot be overestimated in bringing an ideal element into our hitherto prosaic New England life.

The seeds of this intellectual growth came suddenly, as if blown from some far-off cultured land, and were sown broadcast. Some found a resting-place in this little corner of New England, where were gathered together these daughters of Puritan ancestors, and they, too, feeling the intellectual impetus, were impelled to put in writing their own crude thoughts. Their desire for self-improvement had been to some extent gratified, and they now began to feel the benefit of the educational advantages which had been opened to them. As in "Mary Barton," they "threw the shuttle with increasing sound, although Newton's 'Principia' lay open before them, to be snatched at in work-hours, but revelled over at meal-time or at night."

And the "literary" girls among us would often be seen writing on scraps of paper which we hid "between whiles" in the waste-boxes upon which we sat while waiting for the looms or frames to need attention. Some of these studious ones kept note-books, with abstracts of their reading and studies, or jotted down what they were pleased

to call their "thoughts." It was natural that such a thoughtful life should bear fruit, and this leads me to speak of
The Lowell Offering, a publication which was the natural
outgrowth of the mental habit of the early mill-girls, for
many of the pieces that were printed there were thought
out amid the hum of the wheels, while the skilful fingers
and well-trained eyes of the writers tended the loom or
the frame.

The idea of organization for literary and educational
purposes was first proposed in 1837 by Miss Harriot F.
Curtis, perhaps the most progressive of all the mill-girls.
She with her immediate associates conceived the idea of
forming a little society for mental improvement. In *The
Lowell Offering* of January, 1845, is the following account
of its formation written by Miss Maria Currier.

"IMPROVEMENT CIRCLE.

"In one of the corporations [the Lawrence] of this city, about
eight years ago, might have been seen, on a summer evening, a
company of four or five young females, who through the day had
labored at their several employments in some one of the factories
connected with the corporation. Perhaps they were not ambitious
above others of their sex.... But wishing to improve the talents
which God had given them, they proposed the formation of a
society for mutual improvement. An evening was appointed for
the proposed purpose; and having invited a few others to join
them, they met at the time appointed.... A president, vice-
president, and secretary were chosen; a constitution was drafted,
and by-laws formed, to which each of the members affixed her
name.... At length a circle on a more extensive scale was
formed by a gentleman of this city, and a plan conceived of
bringing before the world the productions of inexperienced females; of showing that intellect and intelligence might be found
even among factory operatives. It was then that *The Offering* was
published; and many of those who were present at the first meeting of our Improvement Circle were contributors to its pages."

At the first meeting, Miss Curtis delivered a stirring
address, in which she stated the object and scope of the organization, and the urgent need that existed for all working-women to make an effort to improve their minds.

The club met fortnightly, and each member contributed
articles in prose and verse, which were read at the meetings, and subjected to the criticism of those present.

In answer to a letter of enquiry, Miss Curtis writes: "I do not remember who composed the first circle, not even the names of the officers; but I think Emmeline Larcom was secretary. Farther than that I can only say, I was not anything. I never would hold any office,—office brings trammels. I believe I wrote and read the address of which Maria speaks. Louisa and Maria Currier, Emmeline Larcom, Harriet Lees, and possibly Ann Carter were there.... If you want to know whose brain conceived the idea, I suspect it was I. I was always daring; the other five were modest and retiring." And thus was formed the first woman's literary club in this country,—a remote first cause of the hundreds which now make up the General Federation of Women's Clubs, since it bears the same relation to that flourishing institution as the native crab does to the grafted tree. Some of these early club, or improvement circle women either are, or have been, members of similar organizations in the localities in which they live, and have done their best to incorporate into the constitution of the modern woman's club the idea of "improving the talents God has given them." And if they have continued to live up to this doctrine, no doubt they have attained, if not to all they may have desired, at least to all they were capable of achieving, according to their limitations.

It may be well to mention here that Improvement Circles continued to be formed, and that in 1843 there were at least five in different parts of the city. I attended one in 1845, connected with *The Lowell Offering*. It met in the publication office, on Central Street, and was well filled with factory operatives, some of whom had brought their contributions, and waited to hear them read, with quaking hearts and conscious faces. Harriet Farley presided, and from a pile of manuscript on the table before her selected such contributions as she thought the most worthy of a public reading. Among these, as I remember, were the chapters of a novel by Miss Curtis, one of Lucy Larcom's prose poems, and some "pieces of poetry." Included in these pieces were some verses in which the wind was

described as playing havoc with nature to such an extent
that—

"It took the tall trees by the hair,
And as with besoms swept the air."

This tremendous breeze, or simile, caused a good deal of
mirth among the younger contributors, who had never
heard of "The World-Soul," nor read Emerson's line—

"To the green-haired forest free,"

nor Longfellow's "The Building of the Ship," where he
speaks of the pine-trees as—

"Shorn of their streaming hair."

Nor yet Wordsworth's sonnet:—

"While trees, dim seen, in frenzied numbers tear
The lingering remnant of their yellow hair."

This was my only appearance at the Circle, as I had
hitherto been deterred from going by the knowledge that
those who went were expected to bring a written contribution to be read there. Shortly after this, Miss Farley
(one of the editors) invited me to send something to the
magazine, and I complied; but I was not an early or a
constant contributor.

In 1839, the Rev. Abel C. Thomas and the Rev. Thomas
B. Thayer, pastors of the First and Second Universalist
Churches in Lowell, established improvement circles composed of the young people belonging to their respective
parishes. These meetings were largely made up of young
men and women who worked in the mill. They were often
asked to speak; but as they persistently declined, they
were invited to write what they desired to say, and send
it, to be read anonymously at the next meeting. Many of
the young women complied with this request, and these
written communications were so numerous that they very
soon became the sole entertainment of what Mr. Thomas
called "these intellectual banquets."

A selection from the articles read at these meetings
was published by Mr. Thomas in pamphlet form, under
the title, *"The Lowell Offering,* a Repository of Original

articles written by Females employed in the Mills." Mr. Thomas's own account of his part in establishing the magazine will be found in chapter seven. The first series, of four numbers, was issued from October, 1840, to March, 1841; and there was such a demand for copies, that a new series began. *The Lowell Offering* proper, a monthly magazine of thirty-two pages, which was issued regularly by its projector from that time until October, 1842, when it passed into the hands of Miss Harriot F. Curtis and Miss Harriet Farley, both operatives in the Lowell mills.

Under their joint editorship it was published, the first year by William Schouler, but after that by these ladies themselves, who were editors, publishers, and proprietors, until December, 1845, when, with the end of Volume V, Miss Curtis retired from the magazine, and *The Lowell Offering* ceased to exist.

But in September, 1847, Miss Farley resumed the publication of the magazine and issued one copy under the title *The New England Offering;* and all those who were or had been factory operatives were invited to contribute to its pages.

This magazine was re-issued in 1848, from April to December, continued through 1849, and until March, 1850, when it was discontinued for want of means, and perhaps new contributors. Miss Farley was the editor, publisher, and proprietor of *The New England Offering.*

There are about seven volumes of the magazines in all,—five of *The Lowell Offering,* and two of *The New England Offering,* including the first four numbers in 1840, and the odd numbers of 1847 and 1850.

The prospectus of *The Lowell Offering,* as issued by its women-editors in 1845, is as follows:—

THE

LOWELL OFFERING,

WRITTEN, EDITED, AND PUBLISHED

BY FEMALE OPERATIVES.

OUR magazine is the only one which America has produced, of which no other country has produced the like. *The Offer-*

ing is *prima facie* evidence, not only of the American "factory-girls," but of the intelligence of the mass of our country. And it is in the intelligence of the mass that the permanency of our republican institutions depends.

And our last appeal is to those who should support us, if for no other reason but their interest in "the cultivation of humanity," and the maintenance of *true* democracy. There is little but this of which we, as a people, can be proud. Other nations can look upon the relics of a glory come and gone—upon their magnificent ruins—upon worn-out institutions, not only tolerated, but hallowed because they are old—upon the splendors of costly pageant—upon the tokens of a wealth, which has increased for ages—but we can take no pride in these. We have other and better things. Let us look upon our "free suffrage," our Lyceums, our Common Schools, our Mechanics' Literary Associations, the Periodical of our Laboring Females; upon all that is indigenous to our Republic, and say, with the spirit of the Roman Cornelia, These, these are our jewels.

TERMS: One dollar per year in advance. POSTAGE: : 100 miles and under, 1½ cents. Over 100, 2½ cents.

Published at Lowell, Mass., monthly, by
MISSES CURTIS & FARLEY.

In order to combat the prejudice which then existed against "female" editors and publishers, it was thought best (as Mr. Thomas had advised) that the enterprise should be indorsed by some of the leading men of the city; and in the original document, now before me, these gentlemen said:—

"We wish herewith to express most cheerfully our confidence in their talents and moral worth, and our cordial approbation of the worthy enterprise in which they are engaged.... We wish only to witness to any to whom this may come, that Miss Harriet Farley and Miss Harriot Curtis are worthy of entire confidence and are deserving for themselves and for their enterprise the hearty support and encouragement of every lover of his country, of every philanthropic citizen. We shall always rejoice to hear of their success.

(Signed by)

SAMUEL LAWRENCE,
BENJ. F. FRENCH,
J. W. WARREN,
WILLIAM BUTTERFIELD,

JOHN CLARKE,
HOMER BARTLETT,
WILLIAM SCHOULER,
JACOB ROBBINS,

JOHN AVERY,   GEORGE MOTLEY,
ALEXANDER WRIGHT,   WILLIAM SPENCER,
JOHN WRIGHT.
LOWELL, *Nov.* 25, 1843

It may be well to record the fact, that at this date, according to the *Lowell Journal,* there were only three women editors in this country besides Miss Curtis and Miss Farley. These were Cornelia W. Walter of the *Boston Transcript,* Mrs. Green of the *Fall River Wampanoag,* and Lydia Maria Child of *The Anti-Slavery Standard.*

In an editorial notice of all these women editors, the *Journal* says, "*The Anti-Slavery Standard,* edited by Lydia Maria Child, is one of the best papers in the country.... We do not doubt that the women will have a good influence in this new sphere, as they do in everything else;" and continuing, "*The Lowell Offering* must be made the instrument of great good. In glancing at its contents and reflecting upon the origin of its articles, our respect for woman and her saving and regenerating power is increased a thousand fold."

In order to keep the continuity of the literary history of the early working-girls, it is well to speak of a contemporary publication called *The Operatives' Magazine,* published in Lowell by "an association of females," and edited by Lydia S. Hall and Abby A. Goddard, both factory-girls. The leading editorial stated that "The magazine will contain original articles on religious and literary subjects," and added that "Those which inculcate the doctrines of the Bible as understood by evangelical Christians, without their peculiarities, will be admitted." Contributions were solicited from "operatives of both sexes."

This magazine was published in 1841–1842, when it was merged in *The Lowell Offering.* Lucy Larcom and her sister Emmeline were contributors, during its existence, to *The Operatives' Magazine,* which may account for the fact that Lucy Larcom did not write for *The Lowell Offering* (with the exception of some verses in the first series) while it was under the control of Mr. Thomas; but she became a constant contributor after that date, both to *The Lowell Offering* and to *The New England Offering.*

CHAPTER VII.

THE LOWELL OFFERING (CONTINUED).

The Lowell Offering was a small, thin magazine of about thirty pages, with one column to the page. The price of the first number was six and a quarter cents. Its title-page was plain, with a motto from Gray; the verse beginning:—

"Full many a gem of purest ray serene."

This motto was used for two years, when another was adopted:—

"Is Saul also among the prophets?"

In January, 1845, the magazine had on its outside cover a vignette, a young girl simply dressed, with feet visible and sleeves rolled up. She had a book in one hand, and her shawl and bonnet were thrown over her arm. She was represented as standing in a very sentimental attitude, contemplating a beehive at her right hand. This vignette was adopted, as the editor said, "To represent the New England school-girl, of which our factories are made up, standing near a beehive, emblem of industry and intelligence, and in the background the Yankee schoolhouse, church, and factory." The motto was:—

"The worm on the earth
May look up to the star."

This rather abject sentiment was not suited to the independent spirit of most of the contributors, who did not feel a bit like worms; and in the February number it was changed to one from Bunyan:—

"And do you think the words of your book are certainly true?
"Yea, verily."

The magazine finally died, however, under its favorite motto:—

"Is Saul also among the prophets?"

The title-page, or outside cover, was copyrighted in 1845. *The Lowell Offering* was welcomed with pleased surprise. It found subscribers all over the country. *The North American Review,* whose literary *dictum* was more autocratic than it is to-day, indorsed it, and expressed a fair opinion of its literary merit.

The editor, John G. Palfrey, said:—

"Many of the articles are such as to satisfy the reader at once, that if he has only taken up *The Offering* as a phenomenon, and not as what may bear criticism and reward perusal, he has but to own his error, and dismiss his condescension as soon as may be."

Charles Dickens, in his "American Notes," says:—

"They have got up among themselves a periodical, called *The Lowell Offering,* whereof I brought away from Lowell four hundred good solid pages, which I have read from beginning to end. Of the merits of *The Lowell Offering,* as a literary production, I will only observe—putting out of sight the fact of the articles having been written by these girls after the arduous hours of the day—that it will compare advantageously with a great many English annuals."

Harriet Martineau prompted a fine review of it in the London *Athenoeum,* and a selection from Volumes I. and II. was published under her direction, called "Mind Among the Spindles."

This book was issued first in London, in 1844, and republished in Boston in 1845, with an introduction by the English editor, Mr. Knight. In a letter to this gentleman, Miss Martineau said, "I had the opportunity of observing the invigorating effect of 'Mind among the Spindles,' in a life of labor. Twice the wages and half the toil would not have made the girls I saw happy and healthy, without that cultivation of mind which afforded them perpetual support, entertainment, and motive for activity. They were not highly educated; but they had pleasure in books and lectures, in correspondence with home, and had their minds so open to fresh ideas as to be drawn off from thoughts of themselves and their own concerns."

English friends were particularly kind in their expressions of approval. One said, *"The Lowell Offering* is probably exciting more attention in England than any other American publication. It is talked of in the political, as well as in the literary world.... It has given rise to a new idea, that there may be mind among the spindles .... The book is a stubborn fact."

President Felton of Harvard University, while in Paris attending a course of lectures on English Literature by Philarète Chastles, heard an entire lecture on the history and literary merits of *The Lowell Offering*.

Thiers, the French historian, carried a volume into the Chamber of Deputies, to show what working-women in a republic could do.

George Sand (Madame Dudevant) thought it a great and wonderful thing that the American mill-girls should write and edit a magazine of their own.

Chambers's Edinburgh Journal gave *The Offering* a rather *back-handed* compliment, which is quoted to show the old-time prejudice against *female* writers. It said,—

"Constrained to speak candidly, we have found amongst the pieces few which would have any chance of admission into a British periodical above the humblest class; yet it must also be admitted, that even where there is no positive attraction, there is nothing irreconcilable with good taste; and some of the articles, the verse as well as the prose, would appear as respectable efforts for females of any rank in life."

It may be said that at one time the fame of *The Lowell Offering* caused the mill-girls to be considered very desirable for wives; and that young men came from near and far to pick and choose for themselves, and generally with good success. No doubt these young men thought that, if a young woman had the writing talent, rare in those days, she naturally would have other rare talents towards the making of a good wife; and I can say that my own knowledge, added to recent inquiries, confirms this belief.

The fact was often disputed that a "factory-girl" could write for or edit a magazine, since she had hitherto been considered little better than the loom or frame she tended. Inquiries on the subject came to the editors from different parts of the country, and questions like the following were often put to them: "Do the factory-girls really *write* the articles published in *The Offering?*" or, "Do you print them just as they are sent?" or, "Do you revise or rewrite them?"

In the preface to the first volume, Mr. Thomas answered these questions. He says, "The articles are all written by factory-girls, and *we do not* revise or re-write them. We have taken less liberty with them than editors usually take with other than the most inexperienced writers." He adds, "Communications much amended in process of training the writers were rigidly excluded from print; and such articles only were published as had been written by females employed in the mills." He continues, "and thus was published not only the first work written by factory-girls, but also the first magazine or journal written exclusively by women in all the world."

The contributions to *The Offering* were on a great variety of subjects. There were allegories, poems, conversations on physiology, astronomy, and other scientific subjects, dissertations on poetry, and on the beauties of nature, didactic pieces on highly moral and religious subjects, translations from French and Latin, stories of factory and other life, sketches of local New England history, and sometimes the chapters of a novel. Miss Curtis, in 1840, wrote an article on "Woman's Rights," in which were so many familiar arguments in favor of the equality of the sexes, that it might have been the production of the pen of almost any modern advocate of woman's rights; but there was this difference, that the writer, though she felt sure of her ground, was too timid to maintain it against the world, and towards the end throws out the query, "whether public life is, after all, woman's most appropriate and congenial sphere?" It is a curious coincidence, that at this date the English and the American Anti-Slavery Associations were at the point of division on this very question.

There is a certain flavor in all *The Lowell Offering* writings, both in prose and verse, which reminds one of the books read by the authors, and the models they followed in their compositions. The poetry savors of Mrs. Sigourney, Mrs. Hemans, Miss Landon, Mrs. Barbauld, Milton, Pope,

Cowper, and Hannah More. Byron's sardonic vein is copied by one or two of the most independent minds among them. The prose models of writing were *The Spectator,* the English classics, "Miss Sedgwick's Letters," "The Vicar of Wakefield," and Lydia Maria Child's writings.

Though the literary character of these writings may not rise to the present standard of such productions, yet at that season of intellectual dearth they must have had a certain influence on contemporary literature; and viewed by the critical eye of a later date, it is found that the selections from *The Lowell Offering* will compare quite favorably with those in the "Ladies' annuals" of the same date, as, for instance, *The Lady's Repository, The Rose of Sharon, The Lily of the Valley, Gems of Beauty, The Opal,* and other like literary curiosities, of which *The Lowell Offering* may well be ranked as one, and with which, no doubt, it will hold its place in the history of American publications.

These factory-girl writers did not confine their talents within the pages of their own publication. Many of them wrote for the literary newspapers and magazines. One sometimes filled the poet's corner in *Zion's Herald* and in the *Saturday Evening Gazette;* another took that envied place in *The Ladies' Casket;* a third sent poetic effusions to *The Lowell Courier and Journal.*

These authors represent what may be called the poetic element of factory-life. They were the ideal mill-girls, full of hopes, desires, aspirations; poets of the loom, spinners of verse, artists of factory-life.

The Lowell Offering did a good work, not only among the operatives themselves, but among the rural population from which they had been drawn. It was almost the only magazine that reached their secluded homes, where it was lent from house to house, read and re-read, and thus set the women to thinking, and added its little leaven of progressive thought to the times in which it lived. Its influence or its memory is not by any means forgotten; and if a newspaper or magazine which had so brief an existence is so well remembered after at least fifty years, when

the novelty of such a publication is all worn away, it shows
that it must have had some vitality, something in it worthy
of preservation.

It was considered good Sunday reading. A friend told
me recently that as a child she used to watch for its coming, and how much she liked it, because her father, a
clergyman, allowed her to read it on Sunday; and on that
day it was placed on the table with the Bible, while other
secular reading-matter was excluded. Another has said
that she used to get the themes for her "compositions"
out of the pages of *The Lowell Offering.*

The names of the *Lowell Offering* writers, so far as I
have been able to gather them, are as follows: Sarah G.
Bagley, Josephine L. Baker, Lucy Ann Baker, Caroline
Bean, Adeline Bradley, Fidelia O. Brown, M. Bryant, Alice
Ann Carter, Joanna Carroll, Eliza J. Cate, Betsey Cham-
berlain, Lucy A. Choate, Kate Clapp, Louisa Currier, Maria
Currier, Lura Currier, Harriot F. Curtis, Catherine Dodge,
Eliza B. Dodge, M.A. Dodge, Harriet Farley, Margaret F.
Foley, A.M. Fosdick, Abby A. Goddard, M.R. Green, Lydia
Sarah Hall, Jane B. Hamilton, Harriet Jane Hanson, Ra-
chel Hayes, Eliza Rice Holbrook, Eliza W. Jennings, Han-
nah Johnson, E. Kidder, Miss Lane, Emmeline Larcom,
Lucy Larcom, L.E. Leavitt, Harriet Lees, Mary A. Leonard,
S.G. Lyon, Helen A. Macdonald, Sarah E. Martin, Mary
J. McAffee, A.E.D. Perver, E.S. Pope, Nancy R. Rainey,
Sarah Shedd, Hellen E. Smith, Ellen M. Smith, Laura
Spaulding, Mary Ann Spaulding, Emmeline Sprague, S.W.
Stewart, Laura Tay, Rebecca C. Thompson, Abby D. Turn-
er, Elizabeth E. Turner, Jane S. Welch, Caroline H. Whit-
ney, A.E. Wilson, Adeline H. Winship, and Sabra Wright,
sixty-two in all.

Most of the writers signed fictitious names, such as Ella,
Adelaide, Dorcas, Aramantha, Stella, Kate, Oriana, Ruth
Rover, Ione, Dolly Dindle, Grace Gayfeather, and many
others.

In 1848 seven books had been published, written by
contributors to *The Lowell Offering.* These were "Lights
and Shadows of Factory Life," and "Rural Scenes in New

England," by Eliza Jane Cate; "Kate in Search of a Husband," "Jessie's Flirtations," and "S.S.S. Philosophy," by Harriot F. Curtis; "Domestic Sketches" by Abby A. Goddard, and "Shells from the Strand of the Sea of Genius" by Harriet Farley.

Not many of the lesser lights continued to write after their contributions were no longer in demand for *The Offering.* But there were a few who had written for the pure love of it, and who, in spite of their other duties, and a restricted life, still clung "to the dreams of their youth," and kept up the writing habit, even beyond the verge of the allotted threescore years and ten.

There is hardly a complete set of *The Lowell Offering* in existence. I have Miss Larcom's copies, which, added to my own, the result of many years of collecting, in the shape of gifts, make as complete a set as I have been able to find. The 1847 copy I never heard of outside my own collection. Mr. C.F. Libbie of Boston has nearly a full set, with a rare collection of bibliology relating to the magazine.

The volumes in the State Library are neither perfect nor consecutively bound. A set of *The Lowell Offering,* complete to 1847, was sent by the mayor of Lowell to the mayor of Paris, "all neatly bound and lettered."

There are odd volumes, no doubt, in libraries or in private collections, but they are not complete enough to give an adequate idea of the magazine; and unless such a book as this were written, an historical record of what is now considered a most interesting phase in the history of early factory labor would not be preserved. I may add to this, that the Lowell Public Library contains the first five volumes, which are *The Lowell Offering* proper. In closing this brief sketch of *The Lowell Offering,* it may be well to quote Mr. Thomas's letter, written to the *Vox Populi,* Lowell, in answer to a request for information with regard to his connection with the magazine.

Dear Sir,—Your letter of December 9th, 1872, solicits me to furnish, in some detail, the facts, as I now remember them, respecting the origin and early history of *The Lowell Offering,* the writers for it, etc.

It would seem, by your epistle, that you have seen, and perhaps own, the second and later series of the unique publication, but that you question whether a copy of the first four numbers is in existence—indicating, I judge, that you have sought for them in vain.

I am happy to inform you that your apprehension of total loss is "ruled out" by my possession of two complete sets of those first four numbers, lacking only the printed cover of Number One. You will not be surprised that my sons, to whom they belong, are unwilling to part with these memorials of their father's brief residence in Lowell; but I hope that your earnest antiquarian call will awaken a response among the hidden or forgotten things of some one of your many readers.

Meanwhile I will endeavor to make a compact statement of what you desire, with no more of personality than is necessary to an intelligible narrative.

Number 1 of *The Lowell Offering* was published in October, 1840. No. 2 was issued in December following. No. 3 appeared in February, 1841, and No. 4 in March. Printed by A. Watson, 15 Central Street. Each number consisted of sixteen pages small quarto, double columns, in small pica solid, and was sold at retail for six and one-fourth cents. I have forgotten how many copies were printed. The third and fourth pages of a plain cover were devoted to advertisements of less than an average of one inch brevier, and in this way we managed to 'make both ends meet.'

In No. 2 appeared the following note, the words in brackets being here inserted in the way of explanation.

"A social meeting, denominated Improvement Circle, was established in this city about a twelve-month since [by the Rev. A.C. Thomas, pastor of the Second Universalist Church]. At the sessions of this Circle, which have been holden one evening in a fortnight, communications (previously received by the gentleman in charge) have been read, the names of the writers not being announced. The largest range of subject has been allowed;... The reading of these articles has constituted the sole entertainment of the meetings of the Circle. The interest thus excited has given a remarkable impulse to the intellectual energies of our population.

"At a social meeting for divine worship connected with one of our societies (First Universalist Church, the Rev. T.B. Thayer, pastor), communications, chiefly of a religious character, have been read, during several years past ....

"A selection from the budgets of articles furnished to these Circles, together with a few communications derived from other sources, constitutes *The Lowell Offering,* whereof the two gentlemen in charge of the meetings aforesaid are the editors.

"We have been thus particular, partly to gratify the curiosity of our readers, and partly to call attention to the advantage of such social institutions for improvement in knowledge, and in the art of composition. The meetings being free to all who are disposed to attend, they may be likened to so many intellectual banquets, the writers furnishing the feast of reason, while all present participate in the flow of soul."

Confessedly there was little novelty in the organization and conduct of these Circles, excepting perhaps that the leaders took special pains in private interviews, and by informal hints and criticisms at the gatherings, to awaken and foster a desire for improvement. But the honorable presentation to the world, in print, of a class of people usually considered ignorant and degraded, was certainly a new thing under the sun.

In the number of *The Offering* for November, 1842, which was after my removal from New England, Miss Harriet Farley, who was then in editorial charge, published her personal knowledge of the origin, etc., as follows:—

"The gentlemen were at liberty to contribute to the Circle, but they were of no great assistance. Those who were not engaged in the mills were also contributors, but it was soon found that the principal interest of the meetings depended upon *the factory-girls.*

... "There were at length so many articles of a promiscuous character, that it was thought they might form a pleasing variety in a little book.... To tell the truth, we did not really believe that it would ever come into being. We did not believe our articles would do to print—that they were good enough to be put in a book. But there was *one* who thought otherwise.... Then a periodical was spoken of, and it was even suggested that *we* should edit it. *We* the editor! The idea was very awful. *We* should as soon have thought of building a meeting-house! We shrank so sensitively from the proposal that it was not urged, and the projector of the work became its editor.

"We shall never forget our throb of pleasure when we first saw *The Lowell Offering* in a tangible form, with its bright yellow cover, nor our flutterings of delight as we perused its pages. True, we had seen or heard the articles before, but they seemed so much better in print! They appeared to be as good as anybody's writings. They sounded as if written by people who never worked at all.

"*The Offering* was well received by the public, or at least would have been if people had not been so confused and perplexed and mystified and unbelieving.

"The first number was an experiment, and a successful one. The second, third, and fourth appeared at irregular intervals;

and then it was thought best that it should be permanently established. Hitherto it had been sold singly, or given away, and there
had been no subscription list. With the fifth number commenced
a new series, different in form and materially improved in out-
ward appearance."

The new series was a monthly of thirty-two pages, large oc-
tavo, in long primer, leaded, with embellishments of wood en-
gravings, chiefly of churches in Lowell, also pages of music,
the whole put up in neat printed covers.

Communications much amended in the process of training
the writers were rigidly excluded from print, and such articles
only were published as had been written by females employed
in the mills. One article only was afterwards challenged as a
plagiarism. A few of the contributions from the first needed only
the usual corrections to fit them for the press; the contributors,
besides possessing rare native talent, having had the advantages
of a New England common-school education.

Mostly the writers chose to appear anonymously, not subscribing even their initials; and I am not at liberty to reveal
their names, even if I could remember and designate them all.
I have, however, already mentioned Miss Harriet Farley, and
may add that she was a daughter of the Rev. Stephen Farley,
an aged Unitarian clergyman residing in Amesbury, Mass., a man
richer in faith and life than in dimes and dollars. She left home,
and worked steadily in the mills at Lowell, that she might help
a brother through college. I have no hesitation in naming her
as a sample of extraordinary genius. She greatly enriched the
Circle which was in my charge, and was foremost in every issue
of *The Offering* for several years.

Miss Lydia S. Hall was another contributor whose productions
aided largely in the celebrity of *The Offering,* especially in the
line of poetry. "The Tomb of Washington," "Lowell, a parody on
Hohenlinden," "No," and a number of other poetical articles
of singular merit, stamped this "Adelaide" as a remarkable
writer.

Mrs. Betsey Chamberlain, a widow who worked in the mills
for the support and education of her two children, was a constant
Circle helper, and vitalized many pages of *The Offering* by humorous incidents and the wit of sound common sense.

Miss Harriot Curtis, who held a dashing pen, left the mills for
a season to attend to a sick friend in Troy. At the date of her
return, the contents of the second volume of *The Offering* had
already been made up, whereupon, by my encouragement (suggestion, I believe) she wrote a novelette entitled "Kate in Search
of a Husband," the manuscript of which I sold in her behalf to
J. Winchester, a New York publisher, who issued large editions
of it. A year or two later she was associated with Miss Farley

as editor and proprietor of *The Offering*. Several "Chapters on the National Sciences" were written by a factory-girl (Eliza J. Cate) in Manchester, N.H. She afterwards wrote "Lights and Shadows of Factory Life," also "Rural Life in New England," both of which I sold to Winchester in her behalf.

On the second page of the cover of Number 4, issued March 4, 1841, an endeavor to establish *The Offering* permanently was announced. "Be the number large or small who are disposed to patronize the undertaking, we have concluded to hazard the experiment for one year," the labor and responsibility being wholly my own.

If my ecclesiastical connections had been of the popular order, there could have been no doubt of success; but I was well known as a Universalist. Sectarian hostility, in that day, was of a sort which would not be tolerated now; and I had to combat the falsehood that *The Offering* was a Universalist publication.

The Operatives' Magazine was issued as a rival, or competitor; and only the superior talent of the contributors to the original work kept it in the ascendant of repute and circulation...

I have thus endeavored to answer your inquiries, and will add a few incidents.

In January, 1842, Samuel Lawrence introduced me to Charles Dickens, who was at that time on a tour of inspection in Lowell. In a brief interview, I gave him assurance that all the articles in *The Offering* were written by the class known as factory-girls. I afterward sent him a bound copy of the first volume, new series, which he noticed at some length in "American Notes for General Circulation."

A volume entitled "Mind among the Spindles," being a selection from *The Offering*, was published in England under the auspices, I believe, of Harriet Martineau. She, at all events, was the prompter of a fine review in *The London Athenaeum*. This was early in 1843. The compliment was acknowledged by the present of an elegantly bound copy of the first and second volumes of the new series, with the inscription:—

"HARRIET MARTINEAU,
FROM
HARRIET FARLEY, HARRIOT CURTIS, AND
HARRIET LEES."

The distinguished authoress said in reply: "It is welcome as a token of kindness and for its own value, and above all as a proof of sympathy between you and me, in regard to that great subject, the true honor and interests of our sex." ...

My administration as editor and publisher ceased with the close of the second volume, the numbers of which, as 'copy' was abundant, having been pushed to completion in advance of regular monthly issues.

And now, after the lapse of more than thirty years of varied experience, I send salutations of grace, mercy, and peace to all, being yet in the flesh, who wished well to that undertaking, and helped it, while I here record happy memories of the friends who have passed behind the veil.

Truly yours,

ABEL C. THOMAS.

TACONY, PHILAD., *Dec.* 29th, 1872."

Although the magazine under its women editors was a continued success, still, to Mr. Thomas, as its projector and first editor, must be given the credit of bringing before the public these productions: and too much honor cannot be awarded to him for believing in the capabilities of the young people under his charge, and for utilizing the talent which he found. But for his Improvement Circle *The Lowell Offering* might never have been heard of; and its writers, if this impetus had not been given to their talents, would never have thought themselves capable of any success in this direction. To improve and cultivate the mind was the injunction urged by this good man upon the working men and women of his time.

The fact that Mr. Thomas was the grandson of a noted Quaker preacher (Abel Thomas) probably accounts for his inheritance of the idea, first promulgated in this country by that sect, that women have the right and the ability to express their thoughts, both in speaking and in writing; and he found in Lowell a good field for the application of this principle.

Although a Universalist minister, he was very fond of the Quaker manner of speech, and used the "thee" and "thou" to the end of his life. He was an eloquent and convincing preacher, and consecrated his whole life to the work of disseminating the doctrines of his denomination. He married the daughter of Judge Strange Palmer, of Pottsville, Penn., and M. Louise Thomas is well known as taking a prominent part in many social and philanthropic reforms; it is to her that I am indebted for the privilege of quoting her husband's letter.

Mr. Thomas died Sept. 28, 1880; but he had lived to rejoice in the result of his enterprise, though he had little thought, perhaps, of what would be the outcome of his efforts to encourage the young people of his church and community. He was a model publisher, since, as two at least of his writers testify, he shared the pecuniary profits of his magazine with its contributors.

CHAPTER VIII.

BRIEF BIOGRAPHIES OF SOME OF THE WRITERS FOR *THE LOWELL OFFERING*.

IT remains for me to give, so far as I have been able to glean them, the life-stories of a few of the most important of these mill-girl writers, some of them brief indeed, others perhaps of wider significance, but all telling a tale of honest toil and earnest aspiration. I begin with Miss Curtis, as senior editor of the magazine.

HARRIOT F. CURTIS,
Editor of the Lowell Offering.

Among all the writers, Miss Curtis stands out as the pioneer and reformatory spirit. She was fearless in her convictions; she wrote in advocacy of the anti-slavery cause when the real agitation had hardly begun, and in behalf of woman's right to "equal pay for equal labor," five years before the first woman suffrage convention was held in this country.

She organized the first known woman's club, and was one of the four women editors of her time. She was the novelist *par excellence* of *The Offering,* and had a bold and dashing pen that would have made her fortune in these days of women reporters and interviewers. But she was so startlingly original in her speech and in her writings, that it "made talk," as Samantha Allen says, so different was she from the established idea of what a "female" should be.

But she was self-centred, and bore with Christian philosophy as well as with pagan silence and stoicism, "the slings and arrows" of those who could not understand her brave and courageous nature.

Her mind was intensely masculine; but her life had all the limitations by which the women of her time were bound, and these prevented her from doing the work for which she was best fitted, and from leading that life of freedom from care which is so necessary to the best literary work.

Through her grandmother, Abigail Stratton (Curtis), Harriot could claim direct descent from Miles Standish.

She was born Sept. 16, 1813, in Kellyvale (now Lowell), Vt., a little post hamlet on the Missisquoi River, completely surrounded by mountain peaks. The lonely and isolated life she was obliged to lead was very distasteful to her, and she early made up her mind to leave her home and seek more congenial surroundings elsewhere. Her father's means were limited; and after exhausting what education could be obtained in the narrow circle in which she lived, she determined to go to Lowell to work in the factory, and thus earn the money necessary for a year's study at some private school or academy.

Previous to her connection with *The Offering,* Miss Curtis wrote many tales and sketches, and also "Kate in Search of a Husband," one of the first of the "popular novels" in this country. Her novel, "The Smugglers," was begun in *The Offering* of November, 1843.

Her connection with *The Offering* lasted three years; and during the last two, besides contributing and editing, she also assumed that part of the business management which necessitated her travelling and canvassing for subscribers; in fact, as she said, she was "the travelling-agent for the firm, and went roaming about the country in search of patrons."

By this means, she not only helped to place the magazine on a paying basis, but made the acquaintance of many distinguished persons. It was chiefly by the efforts of Miss Curtis at this time that *The Lowell Offering* achieved an almost world-wide fame. When at home she resumed her employment in the mill, as harness-knitter on the Lawrence corporation.

Mr. Thomas, in response to a letter from her asking advice with regard to the business affairs of the magazine, replies:—

"Make your terms cash. You will do well to keep constantly

in remembrance that your prosperity almost entirely depends on your individual exertions. Puffing, advertising, scolding, will do little or nothing. *Male* agents will do little or nothing; but if you go as females, with suitable brief papers signed by *eminent men,* to show that you are not imposters, you will do well.... Be careful to guard against the possibility of suspicion. This you can readily accomplish by certificates from Saml. Lawrence, John Clark, and a few other Lowellites, countersigned (if convenient) by the governor, Daniel Webster, etc."

In her valedictory at the close of Volume V., Miss Curtis announces that she severs her connection with *The Offering* for reasons "entirely of a personal nature," and as a parting benison adds: "Friends, Patrons, and Foes (if we have any), may God bless you all with every perfect gift!"

Although her connection with *The Offering* was severed at this date, Miss Curtis remained in Lowell until called away by the illness of her mother. She continued her literary labors for a time, and was a correspondent of several newspapers. Harriot was the friend and correspondent of such men as John Neal, Horace Greeley, Nathaniel P. Willis, and others well known in literary and public life.

She had a taste for politics and wrote intelligently on questions that women were not supposed to understand. She contributed to the *New York Tribune* articles so clear and so caustic, that readers who did not share the common delusion that "H. G." wrote everything in Horace Greeley's paper, thought they must have been written by a *man!*

She was the friend and correspondent of "Warrington" (William S. Robinson), and when he was editor of the *Boston Daily Republican,* she made a prediction worthy of a male political prophet. In a letter dated May 4, 1848, she writes:—

Friend R.,—Probably no doubt exists but *some* self-sacrificing patriot may be found to accept the office of Chief Magistrate.... But who shall be the Whig candidate for this self-sacrifice, seems the most prominent question. A few days since I met Horace Greeley, and, as in duty bound, pronounced to him my *prophecy* of who *could not* be a successful candidate, although, out of the numerous aspirants for the Whig nomination, I could not prophecy who would be successful.... Will you give the public my assurance that *Henry Clay cannot be President of the United States.* I don't care who the Democratic nominee may be; I don't care how divided that party may be in action, nor how great may be the unanimity and enthusiasm of the Whigs; but I repeat, Henry Clay cannot be President....

I now enter upon the most painful part of her story, and I do it with a heavy heart; but I feel obliged to tell it, because it illustrates so well the lives which so many "solitary" women were then forced to lead,—lives of poverty, of self-abnegation, and of unselfishness. And in reading, in her letters to me, the sad record of her struggles, I can truly say, that never in all my life of over seventy years have I known of one so cruelly compelled by circumstances to hide the talent which "God had given her," that she might become the angel of mercy to her suffering and needy relatives.

In the heyday of her literary career, she left the work for which she was the best fitted, to take the sole charge of her blind and aged mother, who lived until 1858, "having suffered all that mortal could suffer." Harriot was her constant attendant day and night, vainly trying, in the mean while, to get some literary work to do at her home to help eke out the narrow income of the family.

Extracts from her letters written to my husband and myself will give some idea of her struggles to obtain remunerative employment.

SUNNY HILL, DRACUT, *Jan.* 7, 1849.

Dear, dear Friends,—Your kind letter reached me on Friday; and if you could imagine the "heaps" of good it did me, you would favor me often with such medicine. Nobody writes to me nowadays, and I am left to my despair and desolation.... Oh dear! what a world this is for poor old maids! but I trust *you* find it quite comfortable and Paradise-like for brides and bridegrooms, God bless them all! and more especially you young ones....I wish you would show me how I could "earn" anything by writing. I cannot find my way only to write a book, be months about it, and then get a whole $100 for it. That don't pay enough for wear and tear of temper.

Later, in 1860, she writes from the family home in St. Albans, Vt.

"Under present circumstances I do not think I could write a leader. I do not know of anything until it is a week or ten days' old, and my only connection with the living world is the *Tribune.* I thank you with all my heart for your kind offer about going to New York, but it would be useless. Greeley's introduction to

Bonner would not do any good. If I could attract notice, kick up a small tempest, I should feel sure of an invitation from Mr. Bonner. But without some notoriety that *has* created comment, the angel Gabriel could not get into the *Ledger*. Without intellectual contact, out of the world, I have grown rusty. A great care, an increasing anxiety, and most painful sympathy for the suffering, have narrowed my thoughts.... If I could get a little good luck—something to feel pleased about—I think I could wake up to anything.... I could not earn a dollar *here* to save my life. Greeley would say, "Yes, you could: there is the needle; that is useful and wanted, though not half paid." Mr. Greeley does not know that even the resource of the "poor shirtmaker" is denied me. I have lost the use of my thimble finger from one of those awful things, a felon; and it is misshapen, bent, and stiffened. I assure you, I have had a *womanly* experience.... You see, I am 'off the track.'"

After 1860 she ceased trying to secure either fame or money by her literary talents; and thereafter, for almost thirty years, she continued to be the nurse and companion of the remaining invalids of the family, thinking, as she always had done, more of their comfort than she did of the loss of fortune and fame.

If she had devoted all her energies to the development of her talent as a novelist, she might have earned a livelihood, and been a continued success,—enough so, at least, to find a place in some of the many volumes of American biography. But she had the conviction that one has no moral right to live for one's self alone; and so she gave her all, and spent her life, in the service of those who needed her help. And though often despondent, and almost despairing, she never lost faith in God, nor in his fatherly care over the most afflicted of his children.

I first knew Miss Curtis in about 1844, when she and Miss Farley lived in what was then Dracut, in a little house embowered in roses, which they had named "Shady Nook." The house was a sort of literary centre to those who had become interested in *The Lowell Offering* and its writers; and there were many who came from places both near and far to call on the editors, and meet the "girls" who by their pens had made themselves quite noted.

But I did not see much of her until 1848, when we became the firm friends and correspondents that we remained until the end of her life. As I remember her at that time, she was of medium height, rather inclined to stoutness, with small, white, well-shaped hands, brown hair, large blue eyes, a small nose, full red lips, white teeth well divided, and a head—well, more than a match for most of the women, if not the men, of her set.

Miss Curtis had many offers of marriage; but she thought it wrong for a woman to marry for a "home," or unless she loved the man with a "love more enduring than life and stronger than death;" and as she did not meet such a man, she could not enter into her ideal marriage. But the friendships she made were warm and lasting, and the friends with whom she was associated have in these pages given their loving tribute to her characteristics and her capabilities.

Miss Curtis's literary efforts may be summed up as follows: first, "Kate in Search of a Husband, a novel by a Lady Chrysalis," published by J. Winchester, New York, and twice in after years by unknown publishers. The authorship of this novel was claimed by one male writer, and another wrote a counterpart, called "Philip in Search of a Wife."

"Kate" was followed by "The Smugglers," the scene of which was laid in her native town, and "Truth's Pilgrimage, His Wanderings in America and in Other Lands," an allegory. Both of these books were published in continued numbers in *The Offering,* and the first-named was copyrighted by a Boston firm in 1844, but was not published.

Her last novel, "Jessie's Flirtations," was published first by George Munro in 1846 and afterwards by the Harpers; and it still holds its place in their "Library of Select Novels." "S.S. Philosophy," her last published book, is full of pithy paragraphs, containing (as her friend "Warrington" said in the *Lowell Journal*) "much that is sensible, sound, and salutary, as well as some considerable that is saucy and sarcastic." She was for three years co-editor of *The Lowell Offering;* in 1854–1855 she was associate editor of the *Vox Populi,* a Lowell newspaper; and she also wrote for many leading journals, notably *The New York Tribune, The Lowell Journal, The Lowell American,* and N.P. Willis's *Home Journal* (N.Y.).

Her *nom de plume,* "Mina Myrtle," first used by her in the newspapers in 1847, became well known; it was afterwards appropriated by another author as "Minnie" Myrtle. (See Wheeler's "Dictionary of the Noted Names of Fiction.")

During her last years Miss Curtis lived on a small farm in Needham, Mass., with her invalid niece, and was cared for and supported by her nephew, George H. Caldwell, brevetted lieutenant-colonel for gallant and meritorious service at Gettysburg, the Battle of the Wilderness, and before Petersburg.

Miss Curtis died in October, 1889, at the age of seventy-six, leaving the invalid niece, who had been her charge for so many years; but her affection for her "Aunt Harriot" was so strong that she died of "no seeming disease" a few weeks after her distinguished relative.

THE CURRIER SISTERS.

These were four sisters, named Louisa, Maria, Lura, and Marcia, and at least three of them wrote for *The Offering.*

They were the daughters of Mr. John Currier of Wentworth, N.H., and members of Mr. Thomas's congregation and of his Improvement Circle. Maria has put on record an authentic account of the first Improvement Circle (quoted elsewhere); but Lura deserves the most extended mention, from the fact that she, as Mrs. Whitney, was the prime mover in establishing a free library in the town of Haverhill, N.H. Mrs. Whitney died before I had thought to write to her for information; but I am able to quote extracts from the following letter, written by her to Mrs. E. E. T. Sawyer, her early work-mate and lifelong friend, on Jan. 19, 1885.

"I think I have told you about the library that I had the honor of starting here about four and a half years ago. Now we are talking about a new library building; and I think we have made a great start, as one man has given us fifteen hundred dollars towards it. ... As far as our library is concerned, I have accomplished what no one else in this place has done before, and I feel amply repaid in the perusal of some of the interesting volumes contained therein."

Mrs. Whitney died April 4, 1889.

ELIZA JANE CATE.

Miss Cate was the eldest daughter of Captain Jonathan Cate, who commanded a company in the war of 1812. She was born in Sanbornton, N.H., in 1812, and soon achieved good rank as a pure, unaffected, and attractive writer. She was most prolific with her pen, and wrote on a large variety of subjects. Her admirers called her "the Edgeworth of New England."

Her contributions to *The Offering,* notably "Susy L——'s Diary," "Lights and Shadows of Factory Life," and "Chapters on the Natural Sciences," were widely read and commended. Her signature was usually "D." She was a contributor to *Peterson's,* over the signature of "By the Author of Susy L——'s Diary," and wrote for *Sartain's* and other magazines.

Her obituary notice, copied from the newspapers, said:—

"Miss Cate was the author of at least eight books, three of which were issued by the Baptist Publication Society of Philadelphia, and two by J. Winchester of New York. She was a corresponding member of the New Hampshire Historical Society. She died in Poughkeepsie, N.Y., in 1884. Miss Cate was retiring in her manner, but was of a genial and confiding nature; and in her character, as well as in her writings, were blended moral purity with the Christian graces."

MRS. BETSEY CHAMBERLAIN.

Mrs. Chamberlain was the most original, the most prolific, and the most noted of all the early story-writers. Her writings were characterized, as Mr. Thomas says, "by humorous incidents and sound common sense," as is shown by her setting forth of certain utopian schemes of right living.

Mrs. Chamberlain was a widow, and came to Lowell with three children from some "community" (probably the Shakers), where she had not been contented. She had inherited Indian blood, and was proud of it. She had long, straight black hair, and walked very erect, with great freedom of movement. One of her sons was afterwards connected with the *New York Tribune.*

HARRIET FARLEY,

Editor of The Lowell Offering and afterwards
of the New England Offering.

From her autobiography, published in Mrs. S.J. Hale's book, "The Woman's Record," about 1848, I am so fortunate as to be able to quote Miss Farley's own words with regard to some of the events of her early life before and during the time of her connection with both the *Lowell* and the *New England Offering.* Miss Farley says:—

"My father is a Congregational minister, and at the time of my birth was settled in the beautiful town of Claremont, N.H. . . . My mother was descended from the Moodys, somewhat famous in New England history. One of them was the eccentric Father Moody. Another [his son] was Handkerchief Moody, who wore so many years 'the Minister's Veil.' . . . My father was of the genuine New Hampshire stock, from a pious, industrious, agricultural people; his brothers being deacons, and some of his sisters married to deacons. . . . His grandmother was eminent for her medical knowledge and skill, and had as much practice as is usually given to a country doctor. His mother was a woman of fine character, who exerted herself and sacrificed much to secure his liberal education. . . . I was the sixth of ten children, and until fourteen had not that health which promises continued life. . . . At fourteen years of age I commenced exertions to assist in my own maintenance, and have at times followed the various avocations of New England girls. I have plaited palm-leaf straw, bound shoes, taught school, and worked at tailoring, besides my labors as a weaver in the factory, which suited me better than any other. After my father's removal to the little town of Atkinson, N.H., he combined the labors of preceptor of one of the two oldest academies of the State with his parochial duties; and here, among a simple but intelligent people, I spent those years which give tone to the female character. . . . I learned something of French, drawing, ornamental needlework, and the usual accomplishments; for it was the design of my friends to make me a teacher,—a profession for which I had an instinctive dislike. But my own feelings were not consulted. . . . This was undoubtedly wholesome discipline; but it was carried to a degree that was painful, and drove me from my home. I came to Lowell, determined that, if I had my own living to obtain, I would get it in my own way; that I would read, think, and *write when I could,* without restraint; that if I did well I would have the credit of it, if ill, my friends should be relieved from the stigma. I endeavored to reconcile them to my lot by a devotion of all my spare earnings to them and their interests. I made good wages; I dressed economically; I assisted in the liberal education of one brother, and en-

deavored to be the guardian angel to a lovely sister.... It was
something so new to me to be praised and encouraged to write that
I was at first overwhelmed by it, ... and it was with great reluc-
tance that I consented to edit [*The Lowell Offering*], and was quite
as unwilling at first to assist in publishing. But circumstances seem
to have compelled me forward as a business woman, and I have
endeavored to *do my duty.* I am now the proprietor of *The New
England Offering.* I do all the publishing, editing, canvassing; and
as it is bound at my office, I can, in a hurry, help fold, cut covers,
stitch, etc. I have a little girl to assist me in the folding, stitching,
etc.; the rest, after it comes from the printer's hand, is all my own
work. I employ no agents, and depend upon no one for assistance.
My edition is four thousand. These details, I trust, are not tedious.
I have given them because I thought there was nothing remarkable
about *The Offering* but its source and the mode in which it was
conducted."

Of her connection with Mr. Thomas's Improvement Circle
and *The Lowell Offering,* Miss Farley has said to a friend:
"The Circle met in the Sunday-school rooms, and they
were not only filled, but crowded. There was a box placed
at the entrance, so that, if preferred, the writers could be
anonymous; and sometimes topics were suggested. It
seemed almost like an insult when Mr. Thomas first offered payment for these little mental efforts of our leisure
hours.

'I can understand this feeling,' he said. 'I was brought up
a Quaker, and my grandfather never took pay for preaching.
The first money that was ever placed in my hands for this
service seemed to burn into my palms.' There was a little
pile, all in gold, left for our share of the profits of the first
series.

"When I first took the editorial position, I left my regular
place to be what is called a 'spare hand.' This gave leisure
for what I had to do, and there never was any difficulty
about contributions. A large bundle of manuscripts left by
Mr. Thomas was never resorted to but when some short
paper was wanted to fill out a vacant space.

"In the printing-office were Messrs. Hull, Stearns, Taylor,
Brown, Livingston and Durgin, always respectful, kind, and
obliging. In the outer office was Mr. W. S. Robinson, afterwards known as 'Warrington.' These men would soon have
discovered if there had been false pretences about the writ-

ers for the magazine."

In 1847 Miss Farley published a selection from her writings in *The Offering,* with other material, entitled "Shells from the Strand of the Sea of Genius;" she is most fully represented in "Mind Among the Spindles." In 1880 she published a volume of Christmas stories.

Miss Farley married Mr. Dunlevy, an inventor, and they had one child, Inez, who married Mr. George Kyle, a humorous writer and comedian, and died in 1890. Mrs. Dunlevy was living in New York in 1898.

MARGARET F. FOLEY.

That broad-browed delicate girl will carve at Rome
Faces in marble, classic as her own.

An Idyl of Work.

From Miss Foley's letters to Lucy Larcom, and the tender recollections of some of her early and lifelong friends, I am able to piece out a short sketch of this pioneer sculptress.

Margaret Foley was born in Canada, but while she was quite young the family moved to the States. When her father died he left some property, and she was educated fully up to the standard of the young women of her day. She taught school, and at one time was preceptress of Westport Academy. While there she boarded in Lowell, and on Saturday afternoons she taught classes in drawing and painting, and among her pupils was Lucy Larcom. She always had a piece of clay or a cameo in some stage of advancement, upon which she worked in spare moments.

While at Westport Academy she modelled a bust of Dr. Gilman Kimball, a distinguished surgeon of Lowell. She began her artistic life without any teaching, by carving small figures in wood, or modelling busts in chalk; and she often gave these as prizes to her pupils.

She went into the factory to work, that she might share the advantages of the society of other girls who were fond of reading and study, and also that she could enable herself to begin her career as a sculptor.

She did not herself consider that her life in the Lowell factory had any great part in her career, although there is not much doubt that she first conceived the idea of chiselling her thought on the surface of the "smooth-lipped shell" amid the hum of the machinery in the cotton-mill.

She worked a year on the Merrimack corporation; her poems for *The Offering* are written from there, and signed M. F. F. She then went to Boston, where she opened a studio. While in Boston she suffered great privations, and earned but a scanty support in carving portraits and ideal heads in cameo; but she worked on hopefully, doing some excellent likenesses, cameos, medallions, and a few busts; among these, one of cabinet size, of Theodore Parker.

Her cameo-cutting was said to be unsurpassed. After seven years of this life, by the aid of kind friends, the wish of her heart was gratified, and she sailed for Rome, where she began to work in larger material, and to make life-size medallion portraits with much success and profit.

She found warm friends there,—Harriet Hosmer, Mrs. Jameson, Mr. and Mrs. S. C. Hall, W. W. Story, and, best of all, William and Mary Howitt.

From "Mary Howitt, an Autobiography," by her daughter, London, 1889, I am able to give a slight glimpse of the last years of Margaret Foley's life. Mrs. Howitt first speaks of her in 1871, as "the gifted, generous-hearted New England sculptress." In June of that year she went with the Howitts to the Tyrol, where, on setting up housekeeping together, Mrs. Howitt says,—

"Margaret Foley, a born carpenter and inventor, set to work and made us all sorts of capital contrivances." She spent several summers at Meran, a residence for invalids, celebrated for its grape-cure. In 1877 she was taken with a stroke of paralysis, the root of the malady being an affection of the spinal cord, was carried from Rome to Meran, and after several months of great suffering she died there, Dec. 7, 1877.

During her illness, says Mrs. Howitt, her physician "ordered us to write to any near friends or relatives she might have, and that, if she had any affairs to settle, it might be done; but dear Peggy had made her will, and we were among her nearest friends."

The friendship of the Howitts for Margaret Foley was very warm and tender; and she found in their true hearts and in their home that rest and refreshment her loving spirit craved, and that true sympathy for her work which is so necessary for the struggling artist.

I first saw Miss Foley in Rome while I was there with my husband in 1874. We had sent her a letter of introduction from Lucy Larcom with a note, and were invited to take tea with her at 53 Via Margutta, her home. She received us in a most cordial New England manner; we were to have visited her studio the next day, but the sudden illness prevented, and we never saw her again. She was then at work on her "Fountain," and spoke of the figures around it as "my children."

In personal appearance she was very attractive. Of a medium-sized, lithe figure, with small, unusually strong hands, a high, broad forehead, which, in connection with her refined features, gave her the stamp of intellectual power, a luxuriant quantity of soft brown hair, the longest and thickest I ever saw, merry blue eyes, and a head as classic and a skin as white as her own beautiful marbles.

Miss Foley's principal sculptures may be classified in the following order: Among her medallions are Theodore Parker, Charles Sumner, Longfellow, Bryant, William and Mary Howitt, Mrs. S. C. Hall, and perhaps others, said to be "full of purity and grace."

Her ideal productions are Jeremiah, a colossal bust; Pasquiccia; The Fountain; The Young Trumpeter; The Timid Bather; Excelsior; The Head of Joshua; Little Orpheus; Cleopatra; Viola; The Flower Girl; Boy and Cid, a life-sized group; The Baby Piper (Little Pan); and doubtless many others which have not come to my notice.

No adequate biography has yet been written of Miss Foley, although it is said that the daughter of Mary Howitt has contemplated such a work. This would certainly be of value, not only as showing how exceptional talent, (if not actual genius), can assert itself in spite of all limitations, but also as a tribute to a rare and aerial personality.

LYDIA S. HALL.

This writer was *the* poet, *par excellence,* of the early volumes of *The Offering;* as Lucy Larcom said, "She was regarded as one of the best writers of verse while I was in Lowell."

"The Tomb of Washington," first printed in No. 1 of the first series of *The Offering,* was thought to be a wonderful production, and was widely copied. She also wrote for that publication "Old Ironsides," a poem widely read and quoted. She left Lowell before 1848, and went as a missionary to the Choctaw Indians, travelling on horseback a greater part of the way, across the unsettled region.

From letters received from Mrs. Harvey Jones, of Compton, Cal., I am able to gather up a few scattered threads in the eventful life of this pioneer Indian missionary. Mrs. Jones says:—

"My dear Mrs. Robinson,—I was associated in missionary work among the Choctaw Indians with Miss Lydia S. Hall. We were together five years, and I learned to regard her as a dear friend; but in some way I have lost all trace of her. Our relations in the missionary work were very pleasant. She was some years my senior, and her riper experience and judgment were invaluable to me. Her work in the Indian Seminary was thorough, and she was regarded as the Choctaw's friend. Of her literary work I know but little. She wrote occasionally for different periodicals. Her contributions to Woodworth's 'Youth's Cabinet' I have specially in mind. . . . Since I lost trace of her, I came across a poem in the *Christian Union,* entitled 'Our Elder Brother.' It was very rich and tender. It was signed 'L. S. H. G.' I did not then know of her marriage; but I said to myself, 'That sounds like Miss Hall.' . . . Her nature was intense and positive, she had high ideals, and she could not always be patient towards what she considered wrong. Hers was a checkered life, from infancy to age. She was born in 1818."

In "border-ruffian" days Miss Hall lived in Kansas, and was an owner of considerable real estate. She lived on the line of emigration, was hostess of a sort of "Wayside Inn," and was sometimes obliged to keep the peace among the lawless men who infested that part of the country. She would have no quarrelling, drinking, nor gambling on her premises. She was well able to enforce these regulations, being a woman of great courage and most commanding presence.

From a newspaper article some years ago, of which I did not preserve the date, I quote the following:—

"A LOWELL FACTORY-GIRL UNITED STATES TREASURER.

"Miss Lydia S. Hall, who is now acting U.S. Treasurer in the absence of the male chief, was once a Lowell factory-girl, and was a contributor to *The Lowell Offering....* Meeting with some misfortune with regard to titles of property, she went to Washington, and has a clerkship in the Treasury Department since, being also engaged in studying law in order to enable her to secure her property rights in Kansas.... She is a lady of great versatility of talent, and would fill a higher position that the one she now occupies with credit."

Miss Hall's letters to Lucy Larcom would have thrown much light on her stirring and eventful life, but these were destroyed before I had thought to ask for them. Her married name was Graffam, but whether she is alive or dead, I do not know.

HARRIET JANE HANSON.

WRITTEN BY LUCY LARCOM.[1]

In these days, when woman's place in the community, as well as in the family, is coming to be acknowledged; when her abilities in every direction find use and scope; when the labor of her hands, head, and heart is everywhere abundantly honored,—it is well for our younger toilers to see what has been accomplished by those who grew up under circumstances more difficult than those by which they are surrounded. Labor has always been honorable for everybody in our steady-going New England life, but it was not as easy for a young woman to put her mental machinery into working order forty years ago as it is now. Her ambition

---

[1] Miss Larcom prepared this sketch for another purpose, two years before she died; and it is substantially the same, with the addition of a few details, which she suggested and permitted me to supply.

for the education of her higher faculties was, however, all the greater for the check that was put upon it by the necessities of a longer day's toil and the smaller compensation of the older time. It is one of the wholesome laws of our nature that we value most that which we most persistently strive after through obstacles and hindrances.

The author of "The New Pandora" is an illustration of what has been done by one such woman, the development of whose mind began as a child in the Lowell cotton-mills. The book is commended by reviewers as an admirably written composition, a beautiful and successful dramatic poem of woman, the result of ripe years of thought.

Mrs. Robinson's maiden name was Harriet Jane Hanson, and she is by "long descent" of good New England parentage. Her father, William Hanson, was descended from the ancestor who first settled in Dover, N.H.—one of a long line of English Quakers. He was a carpenter, and learned his trade of Peter Cudworth, on Merrimac Street in Boston.

Her mother, Harriet Browne, was of Scotch and English descent, her paternal ancestor, in this country, being Nicholas Browne,—always spelled with an *e,*—who was a member of the Great and General Court of Massachusetts from Lynn in 1641, and afterwards from Reading, in 1655–1656, and 1661.

Her great-grandfather, William Browne, of Cambridge, in 1705 sold sixty acres of upland and swamp to Thomas Brattle, Esq., of Boston, Treasurer of the society known as "The President and Fellows of Harvard University;" and on this land many of the Harvard College buildings now stand. He was a soldier in the French and Indian war in Canada.

Miss Hanson's grandfather, Seth Ingersoll Browne, was a non-commissioned captain at the battle of Bunker Hill; and the old "King's arm" he carried on that decisive day is still in the possession of one of his grandsons. He was one of the "Mohawks" who helped to throw the tea into Boston Harbor; and his name is written in marble, among his companions of "The Boston Tea Party," in Hope Cemetery, Worcester, Mass. He is buried in the Granary Burying-ground, in Boston.

Harriet Hanson was born in Boston, Mass., Feb. 8, 1825, and in 1832 removed with her widowed mother and her three brothers to Lowell, where they lived for some years on one of the manufacturing "corporations." Her first attempt at writing for the press was made while she was yet an operative in the Lowell mills, in the "annuals" and newspapers of the time. She was also a contributor to *The Lowell Offering,* and was on intimate terms with its editors and contributors.

In 1848 she was married to William S. Robinson, journalist and parliamentarian, who, as "Warrington," became well known as the war correspondent in the *Springfield Republican,* the *New York Tribune,* the *New York Evening Post,* and in other newspapers. He was also the author of "Warrington's Manual of Parliamentary Law." Mr. Robinson died March 11, 1876. Their children are Harriette Lucy (married Sidney D. Shattuck of Malden, Mass.), Elizabeth Osborne (married George S. Abbott of Waterbury, Conn.), William Elbridge (died young), and Edward Warrington (married Mary E. Robinson of Denver, Col.).

Mrs. Robinson is deeply interested in all the movements which tend to the advancement of women, and uses her pen and her voice freely in their behalf. She was the first woman to speak before the Select Committee on Woman Suffrage in Congress, and has spoken for the cause before the legislature of her own State, where she is not only a citizen, but a *voter* as far as the law allows.

The woman's club movement has always had her firm support; she assisted at the formation of The General Federation of Women's Clubs in 1890, and was a member of its first advisory board; she is a Daughter of the American Revolution, and a member of the N.E. Historic Genealogical Society.

Mrs. Robinson's first published book was "Warrington Pen Portraits," a memoir of her husband, with selections from his writings. She has also written "Massachusetts in the Woman-Suffrage Movement," and "Captain Mary Miller," a drama.

But her best literary achievement in book form is her latest, "The New Pandora," a poem of which any writer might well be proud. There are passages of exquisitely clear-cut poetry in the drama, and gleams of true poetic aspiration lighting up the homely toil of the woman who knows herself not of earthly lineage.

The "Chorus of Ills" beginning their flight is a strong chant, as classical in its strain as some of Shelley's in his imaginative dramas. Indeed, the whole poem is so classically thought out and shaped as to be lifted quite above what is popular in style, and is for that reason less likely to attract the attention it deserves.

Pandora naturally has at first no love for the rude mate to whom she has been assigned, and it is the death of their little child that brings their hearts together in a real human affection. The loss of this little first-born woman child makes a moan of tenderest pathos through the whole poem, and is a most motherly touch, rarely found in poetry; and the feeling colors the whole book. The poem is pervaded with the sacredness of the domestic affections. The style is strong and clear, and one feels, in reading it, a subtle spiritual fragrance, the beauty, the holiness, the immortality, of human love.

To the writer of this brief notice it is pleasant to recall the time when the author of this beautiful poem and herself were children together, school companions and workmates; when an atmosphere of poetry hung over the busy city by the Merrimack, and when its green borders burst into bloom with girlish dreams and aspirations.

Mrs. Robinson celebrated her seventieth anniversary Feb. 8, 1895, at her home in Malden, Massachusetts.

EMMELINE LARCOM.

In Lucy Larcom's touching poem, "My Childhood's Enchantress," will be found a loving tribute to this mother-sister, to whom she owed so much in her youth and all through her life. It was she who first taught Lucy the use of the pen, and encouraged and helped her in all her literary efforts. She was the oldest own sister of Lucy, is the "Emelie" in the "New England Girlhood," and to her Lucy wrote almost her first, certainly her first *printed,* letter, in 1834, just after their mother had moved to Lowell. This is from her autobiography, printed in *The Lowell Offering.* She says:—

"*Dear Sister,*—We have got a sink in our front entry. We live in a three-story brick block, with fourteen doors in it. There is a canal close by. But no more of this. We arrived safe after our fatiguing journey. We are in good health, and hope you enjoy the same blessing."

In writing of her to me, Lucy says:—

"I was transplanted quite early in my childhood, and grew through girlhood and womanhood under her care. The ten or twelve years of my residence there were certainly very important years to me. My natural bent towards literature was more encouraged and developed at Lowell than it would probably have been elsewhere; and I have always called the place a home in remembrance .... We were often writing to each other, and there never was any break to our affection since my childhood. I think she was almost a perfect woman."

I remember Emmeline as a motherly young woman whom the rest of us looked up to, as one much superior to ourselves; and, in recalling her influence over her younger companions, I think she must have done a great deal towards inciting them to learn to think on earnest subjects, and to express their thoughts in writing. She was tall and stately, with curling hair, and was much prettier than Lucy; she had a face full of sunshine, and, like Lucy, the bluest of blue eyes. She was conspicuous among the group of the original writers for *The Lowell Offering,* as well as *The Operatives' Magazine.*

She was an enthusiastic student, reading abstruse books in the intervals of mill-work, and so becoming familiar with mental and moral science; or she would study mathematical problems, of which she usually had one or two pinned up before her, to occupy her thoughts at her daily toil. The Rev. Amos Blanchard, a very scholarly man, said of her that she was the most intellectual woman in his church, of which she was also one of the most faithful and self-sacrificing members, giving herself unreservedly to all good works.

She married the Rev. George Spaulding, and with her husband and her sister Lucy went, in 1846, to Illinois, and spent the greater part of her life there, as a clergyman's wife, useful, happy, and beloved.

She did not write much after her marriage, and, as she said, would not consider herself an "authoress" at all. She died in Newcastle, Cal., July 17, 1892, leaving her husband, one son, and three daughters. The manner of her death was most enviable. As Lucy wrote me, "she made herself ready for church, but it was heaven for her instead."

At my request Lucy wrote to Emmeline, not long before her death, asking for her recollections of *The Lowell Offering* times; and she replied as follows:—

NEWCASTLE, CAL., *May* 27, 1892.

Dear Sister Lucy,—I have been stirring up my treacherous old memory, hoping to respond to the request of Mrs. Robinson for accurate items in regard to the "Improvement Circle of our girlhood." ... I am very sure indeed that I was an interested and original promoter of it. It seems to me that Harriot Curtis might have suggested it. She was the most intellectual person in my circle of acquaintance at that time. We worked in the same room, and near each other, long before the Improvement Circle had an existence.... She was a mental stimulus to me, and we freely discussed all subjects that came to hand. I think ... that Louisa and Maria Currier, who were Universalists, and Laura and Mary Ann Spaulding, who were Baptists, were among the first members. If I recollect rightly, also Abby Goddard and Lydia Hall.... We had essays and discussions. I was not present at the meeting at Mr. Currier's. I think Mr. Thomas was invited there, and the "Circle" was probably invited to meet at the Universalist vestry. The first *Offering* made its appearance soon after.

I had "A Sister's Tomb" and an article commencing, "Oh, you have no soul," and one other, in the first series.

I did not attend any of the meetings at the Universalist vestry, so am unable to say who suggested *The Offering*. I should think it very likely that Mr. Thomas might have been the one to do so. But the writers had been developed before he knew them. I am quite sure he was much interested in it. I remember that he complimented my verses as the gem of the number.... It was very soon after this that some of us began another Circle-meeting in the vestry of the Congregational church; and out of that grew *The Operatives' Magazine....* I think, as you do, that very much has been made of what was to us a mere recreation, and the most natural thing in the world for a circle of wide-awake, earnest girls to do.... Nearly sixty years have passed since those days; but they are pleasant to remember, and I suspect they held the prophecies of many a pleasant future, of which it might be interesting to know the fulfilment. I did think I should be able to do better, and perhaps write a page for Mrs. Robinson; but you see how I have *not* succeeded.... Here endeth, with love,

BIG OLD SISTER EMMELINE.

LUCY LARCOM.

A part of this sketch of Miss Larcom was written by me not long before her death, and submitted to her for her approval. The additions made are extracts from her letters, with my own personal reminiscences.

In response to my letter asking her approval of what I prepared, Miss Larcom wrote:—

"I approve the sketch, and appreciate your way of writing it, though I don't often encourage living obituary notices of myself. What they call 'fame' amounts to so little. But some things about us in it may help others to know.... I am not ambitious to appear in any book; but if I am to be 'written up,' would much rather it would be done by a friend.... I told in 'A New England Girlhood' all I care to tell about my early life. You know something more of me, and you are at liberty to say what you choose. I have tried to make my life count for good to others, and to make my verses an expression of what I am trying to *live.* You once wrote something about me in *The Independent* that was fresh and natural. Why not utilize that? I have done nothing worth speaking of in a literary sense, but I love to write, and I suppose I shall go on trying to express myself in this way always. The material fact that I have never earned more than enough with my pen than to meet, with difficulty, the necessary expenses of living, does not in the least discourage me, or make me willing to write the trash that 'pays.' That is where I am now on the literary question, and that is where I am content to remain."

It was in that early poetic atmosphere when our American bards first began to teach the young people of the time to love poetry for poetry's sake, that Lucy Larcom received the first incentive to her life-work.

Lucy Larcom was born in one of the earliest settled coast towns in the state, Beverly, Mass., March 5, 1824. Her father, Benjamin Larcom, was a sea-captain; he died when she was a child, and her widowed mother, taking with her Lucy and two or three others of her younger children, then removed to Lowell. The year 1835 found her in one of the Lowell grammar schools, where her education went on until it became necessary for her to earn her living, which she began to do very early as an operative in a cotton factory.

In her "Idyl of Work" the mill-life is truthfully portrayed, with the scenery, characteristics, style of life, thought, and aspirations peculiar to New England womanhood of that period.

In writing to me of this book, in 1875, she says, "What do you think of that name for a reminiscence of Lowell life? Of course you won't like it as poetry; and there is not so very much truth in it, except in general outlines of the way of living. I had to write my remembered impressions, and everybody had different ones. The story, such as it is, is manufactured, of course; for I didn't want any personalities, so I haven't even got myself in, that I know of." ...

But it is very easy to detect, in her loving descriptions, many of her young companions, who shared with her the simplicity of those days of toil; and in following with her the career of some of those bright spirits, and watching their success in their varied pathways through life, it is very pleasant for me to be able to corroborate what she has said.

Riches have fallen to the lot of some of those young girls, and to others a degree of distinction in various situations and occupations; but have they not, from their better surroundings, ever looked back, as she does, to those dear old simple days, so full of health and endeavor, so free from care, as among the happiest of their lives? Then, ignorance of the world was bliss, and hope and aspiration reigned supreme.

My first recollection of Lucy Larcom is as a precocious writer of verses in *The Lowell Casket,* where the editor, Mr. George Brown, in his notice of them, said, "They were written by a young lady of thirteen, who was beyond a doubt inspired by the *Nurses,"*—a misprint, of course, for "Muses;" although the author was so young, that the mistake was not so far wrong.

This, however, was not her first attempt at verse-making, since she began to write while a child of seven or eight years, in the attic of her early home in Beverly. The title of these first verses was "A Thunder Storm," and they were read with wonder by her admiring brothers and sisters.

Two pictures of her in that early factory-life remain in my memory. By the Merrimack River, whose romantic banks she loved to describe, on a bridge which crossed a narrow part of the stream, I once passed her, a tall and bonnie young girl, with her head in the clouds. After a little nod of recognition, as I looked up at her,—for, although she was only a year older than I, she was much larger and more mature,—she went on. But to me she seemed so grand, so full of thought, that, with girlish admiration for one who had written *verses,* I forgot my errand, turned, stood still, and thoughtfully watched her out of sight.

Miss Larcom's first work as a Lowell operative was in a spinning-room on the Lawrence corporation where her mother lived. At first she was a "doffer," with the other little girls; after that she tended a spinning-frame, and then worked in the dressing-room beside "pleasant windows looking towards the river." After this she "graduated" into the cloth-room, and it was here that I saw my second picture of her. The cloth-room was considered by some of the mill-girls a rather aristocratic working-place because of its fewer hours of confinement, its cleanliness, and the absence of machinery. In this room the cloth, after it had been finished and cut into thirty or forty yard pieces in the weaving-room was measured on hooks, one yard apart, until the length of each piece was told off. I used often to run in and see her at her work; and to my imaginative eyes she was like a Sibyl I had read of, as with waving arms she told off the yards of cloth in measured rhythm, and it seemed to be verses, and not cloth, that lay heaped up behind her.

The last two years of her Lowell life (which covered in all a period of about ten years), were spent in the same room; the latter part of the time she was the book-keeper, and recorded the number of pieces and bales. Here she pursued her studies, and in intervals of leisure some text-book usually lay open on her desk, awaiting a spare moment.

Lucy Larcom's first contribution to *The Lowell Offering,* "My Burial Place" (written at sixteen), was published in No. 4 of the first series, and was sent to the editor by her sister Emmeline, while Lucy was on a visit to Beverly. With this exception, she was not a contributor to the magazine while it was under Mr. Thomas's editorship. During that time she wrote for *The Operatives' Magazine,* which was published under the supervision of her pastor, the Rev. Amos Blanchard, and which contained only articles written by the young ladies who were members of an Improvement Circle connected with his parish.

It may be said here that, whatever sectarian feeling there may have been between these rival publications, it was not shared by the girls themselves, at least not by Lucy Larcom. She simply and naturally followed the lead of her pastor. After the "orthodox" magazine stopped, and Miss Curtis and Miss Farley took charge of *The Offering,* Lucy became one of the corps of writers; and many of her verses and essays, both grave and gay, can be found in its bound volumes. Her first contribution to Volume Third, "The River," a poem, appeared in October, 1843. She wrote letters from "Looking Glass Prairie," Illinois; and many of her "prose poems," published afterwards as "Similitudes," with several early poems, including a different version of "The Lady Arabella," first appeared in *The Lowell Offering.*

Our friendship began when we were little girls in "pantalets," when we were "doffers" together in the cotton-mill, and was continued to the end of her life. She also became my husband's friend; and during his lifetime she was our frequent guest, and was always "Aunt Lucy" to our children. Mr. Robinson had great faith in her possibilities as a writer, and he published her verses in his newspaper long before they found admittance into the magazines.

It was through him, while he was the reader (or "stopper") for *The Atlantic Monthly,* during Mr. Lowell's editorship, that "The Rose Enthroned" was brought to the notice of the poet, and afterwards admitted into the pages of the magazine. In a letter to Mr. Robinson, Miss Larcom says of this poem: " 'The Rose Enthroned' was written in 1860, and published in June, 1861, through your mediation, you know."

I should be glad to quote freely from her letters, they are so full of friendship and of loving kindness, but must refrain, and give extracts from those only which relate to her personal history.

In a letter written to me at Concord, Mass., in 1857, she says:—

"I was very glad to hear from you, and was particularly interested in your account of the sewing-society [anti-slavery] at R. W. E.—'s [Ralph Waldo Emerson]. Didn't it seem funny to go a-gossiping to the house of the Seer? I don't wonder at your expecting the parrot to talk 'transcendentally.' Did the tea and toast smack of Hymettus? and was there any apple-*sass* from those veritable sops-o'-wine? Attic salt came in as a matter of course. Well, it's a fine thing to be on visiting terms at Olympus. I should like to see the philosopher again. I don't think I should be afraid of him now .... Sometimes I like philosophers, and sometimes I don't. The thing is to *live*. Beautiful theories don't make any of us do that, but the real breath of life from the Infinite Good, which every soul must have for itself, or, fool or philosopher, he is dead as a heap of sand .... I should like to see the hills where huckleberries grow, and the Pond. There never were hills so still and balmy as those." ...

During the war her letters breathe the spirit of "A Loyal Woman's No!" and show, to one that can read between the lines, that she had a personal interest in saying *No* to a lover who seemed to her to be disloyal to his country.

Although a strong abolitionist, and a believer in the political rights of man, regardless of "race, color, or previous condition of servitude," she did not see the justice of woman's claim to equal rights with man. In answer to a letter asking for her help in the suffrage cause, written in 1870, she says:—

"You know I am way behind the times, am not even a 'suffrage woman' yet, though I haven't the least objection to the rest of the women's having it. Don't you see, I'm constitutionally on the fence. . . . I hope your enthusiastic believers will succeed; and if the suffrage comes, as it will, I hope it will be a blessing to everybody. All the people I know and respect seem to be in the movement, and still 'I don't see it.' . . .

Later, in 1888, she writes:—

"I am for human rights for woman. I never did believe in man's claim to dictate to her. But I want to work for her elevation in my own way, so that when she does vote, it will not be a failure. I cannot 'Club,' myself. I am an obstinate old Independent. . . . Men are chivalrous, you know. Do you suppose we women shall be so towards them, by and by, in the women's millenium? Dear me! I like the old slavish bonds, and am perfectly willing men should rule the world yet, heathenish old maid that I am. Now, here I am perplexed with *two* calls to the meeting to consider the matter of women's voting, about which I have never made up my mind, and can't! If I were a property woman, I might." . . .

In writing of her volume of poetical works, published in 1868, Miss Larcom says,—

"I shall send a volume to your other self and you, (how are we to use adjectives in the Women's Rights speech?), not by way of throwing a sop to Cerberus, but because of old friendship, and because I value your candid opinion *and* Warrington's very highly. I am a little more afraid of you than of him,—I remember Gail Hamilton and the wringing-machine. Don't pillory me in a paragraph, will you? nor inspire the pen masculine with a *bon mot* at my expense."

At Miss Larcom's particular request I have refrained from saying more than is necessary of her as a writer for *The Offering*. On her last visit to me, in 1892, while speaking of the material to be used in this book, she asked me not to say too much about her, because, as she said, she was "tired of being always cited as *the* representative of *The Offering* writers, when there were others who wrote and did quite as much, or more, for the magazine than I did."

Miss Larcom is correct here. Her fame was achieved long after she ceased to be a mill-girl; and there were several others, as the sketches will show, who were as good writers, and much better known than herself, when she left the factory. And it is very thoughtful of her to speak a good word for those hitherto forgotten authors, by declining to be made a sort of composite portrait, as representing the best and brightest among them.

In one of her letters she says,—

"Don't you think it is getting a little tiresome, this *posing* as factory-girls of the olden time? It is very much like politicians boasting of carrying their dinners in a tin pail in their youth. What if they did? ... I am proud to be a working-woman, as I always have been; but that special occupation was temporary, and not the business of our lives, we all knew, girls as we were." ...

"I sent you a copy of my 'New England Girlhood,' for old time's sake. Did you receive it? You could write a more entertaining one. Why don't you write a novel? I wish you would write up *The Offering* time, and sketch Harriot Curtis in it. She was unique."

Miss Larcom's writings, all told, never yielded her income enough to live on, even in her modest way. In speaking of this matter in a letter written in February 1891, she says,—

" 'A New England Girlhood' has as yet brought me only about two hundred dollars. How can writers live by writing?"

She was therefore obliged to supplement her literary labors by teaching. She was very prudent in her manner of living, and never, from childhood, really had a home of her own. Towards the last of her life she found herself much cramped for means to secure that rest her tired brain so much needed; and this made the gifts received from her publisher and from her dearly loved Wheaton Seminary pupils, most welcome, and enabled her, during her last illness, to feel a relief from pecuniary anxiety.

If Miss Larcom had not been exceptionally fortunate, not only in her temperament but in her surroundings,— hampered as she was all through her life by want of pecuniary means,—she could not have developed her writing talent so well. She had the rare gift of finding and keeping the right kind of friends, in her own family as well as outside, and these supplied to her life that practical (though not pecuniary) help she so much needed. So her days were free from household and other cares, and when relieved from her duties as teacher, or as editor, her time was free to use in her own chosen way.

In this, her life differed from that of many women writers, who, whether married or not, often have exacting cares which interrupt and hinder the expression of their written thoughts. Miss Larcom did not have that hindrance; and she had the chance through most of her life to carry out her idea, as she expressed it, of "developing the utmost that is in me." She had no family or domestic cares, and her children were all "dream children."

Miss Larcom might have married, once when she was quite young, and again later; but for reasons of her own she declined,—reasons, the validity of which, in one instance at least, I did not see. I have been asked if Mr. Whittier and Miss Larcom were never more than friends. I can truly answer, no. Miss Larcom was the intimate friend of Elizabeth Whittier, the poet's sister, who, as she said, "was lovely in character, and had fine poetic taste."

She often visited their home, and after the death of the sister the friendship with the brother continued. Miss Larcom was Mr. Whittier's assistant in compiling the books of selections which bear his name, and did a great deal of the actual work in collecting material; they were true friends.

In a letter written shortly after his death, she says,—

"I have not spoken of Mr. Whittier going away. You will know that it is a real sorrow to me, and yet a joy that he has entered into a larger life. . . . This imperfect existence of ours *can be* but the shadow of the true life; in that, there is no death." . . .

One of her last letters to me was written from Boston a few weeks before her death, and is as follows:—

Dear H.,—I have been here nearly a month, but have hardly been out at all. I have never been so much of an invalid, and I don't like it. I suppose I have been steadily "running down," the last year or so, but have gone on just as if I were well. Now I am brought to a stop, and am told that I must never do any more hard work. Lack of strength is what I feel most. They tell me that if I will really rest, brain and body, I may yet accomplish a good deal before I die. I do not feel as if I had got through yet; but who knows? I am trying to realize that it does not make much difference what part of the universe we are in, provided we are on the right track upward. Somehow I feel nearer Emmeline and Mr. Whittier,—as if we knew each other better now than before they went away. I should like to leave my life and work here just when I can go on with what is waiting for me elsewhere. But there is a Master of life who takes care of all that.

Ever truly yours,
LUCY LARCOM.

Of her religious life, it may be said that in her early childhood Lucy became a communicant of the Congregational church; but in later years, as her mind broadened, she became deeply imbued with a sense of the divine fatherhood of God, and the impossibility that He would leave one of the souls that He had made to perish eternally, or, as she says, to quote from her "Biography," "After probing my heart, I find that it utterly refuses to believe that there is any corner in God's universe where hope never comes, . . . where love is not brooding, and seeking to penetrate the darkest abyss."

In 1879 she first listened to Phillips Brooks, and his preaching to her "was the living realization of her own thought." She did not give up her Puritanism, but thought she saw, in the belief and service of his church, a new way of finding the right path towards the end of her journey in search of the truth. As she wrote, "It is not *the* church, but only one way of entering Christ's church." Her religious faith was not so much changed as deepened by this departure from some of the old-time beliefs; for, in writing of the matter to me, she said, "I count the faith of my whole life as one."

Miss Larcom partook of the Holy Communion in Trinity Church, Boston, Easter, 1887, and was confirmed March 20, 1890. By this service, she said, her "heart was fixed," and she could think of herself as "avowedly in the visible church." It was after her connection with the Episcopal Church that Miss Larcom wrote her most important religious books, and these embody much of her own thought in matters concerning the deepest spiritual life.

"Similitudes," a collection of prose poems, was published in 1853; and during the remaining years of her life she published and compiled fourteen books in prose and verse. Her last book, "The Unseen Friend," was published in 1893. The above list does not include the two volumes of poetical selections compiled by herself and Mr. Whittier.

A complete edition of "Larcom's Poems" was published by Houghton, Mifflin, and Co., in the Household edition of the poets, in 1884. In writing of this, Miss Larcom, with characteristic modesty, said, "The idea of my being ranked with other American poets."

She was also editor of *Our Young Folks* from about 1865 to 1872.

Although it is probable that Miss Larcom's fame was achieved as an author of verse, yet she was the best satisfied with her prose productions. As she once said to me, "Essay writing would be my choice, rather than any other form of expression."

It is certain that her name will be the longest remembered by her best-known lyric, "Hannah Binding Shoes;" but this was by no means her favorite, nor would she desire to be remembered by it alone, nor to have it considered as one of the best of her poems. And yet it contains the deep pathos and the tragedy that is in the lives of many solitary women, and as long as such exist, the story of "Poor Lone Hannah" will be read and remembered.

"Hannah Binding Shoes" was written shortly after Miss Larcom's return from Illinois, when the great contrast between the rugged seacoast, so familiar to her early years, and the "boundlessness of commonplace," of the level country she had just left, impressed her most vividly. One summer afternoon, in riding through Marblehead, a face at a window riveted her attention, and haunted her for weeks. Meanwhile, the refrain of the lyric, with its peculiar meter, and the face, continually chased each other through her mind, until, to get rid of their importunate presence, she one day sat down, and imprisoned them together in "immortal verse."

Another poem which takes high rank is "The Rose Enthroned," her earliest contribution to the *Atlantic Monthly,* which, in the absence of signature, was attributed to

Emerson. Also, "A Loyal Woman's No," a patriotic lyric that attracted great attention during our Civil War.

It is such poems as these, with her religious writings and her "Childhood Songs," that will make Lucy Larcom's name remembered. And thousands of earnest working-women will thank her for all that she has written, and go on their way refreshed and encouraged by her success and the fulfilment of her aspirations.

In personal appearance Miss Larcom was tall and stately; her hair was wavy and of a light brown color. Her eyes were of a lovely smiling blue, and her whole face was lit by the charm of them. And who that has heard it can forget her musical laugh, so attractive that even strangers would turn and listen to it, or lose the memory of her beautiful smile, so radiant, so illuminating, that lasted even to the end of her life and that left its lingering gleam on her face after it was cold in death, then to be transplanted to that other life because it was a part of her own immortal self!

Her whole atmosphere was full of a benignant interest in those with whom she came into personal relations. She lived up to her profession, both in religion and in ethics, and was a bright example of what a woman can become, who believes that this life is but the beginning of the next, and who takes the higher law for her inspiration and her guide.

She died April 17, 1893, and is buried in Beverly, Mass., her native place. There, by the seashore, where the salt breezes—

"Chase the white sails o'er the sea,"

and linger lovingly over her grave, her tired body finds its earthly resting-place.

Farewell, old friend and work-mate, but not forever; I too have the conviction, the faith, that this is not all of life, but that sometime, somewhere, we shall take up these broken threads, and go on with our appointed work "on the right track upward."

SARAH SHEDD.

Miss Shedd may be called the philanthropist, *par excellence,* of the early mill-girls. Her whole life was one of self-sacrifice. Her early years were devoted to earning money for the support or the education of members of the family; and at its close she bequeathed the sum of $2,500 for the establishment of the free library in her native town of Washington, N.H.

Her parents were in narrow circumstances; but they had endowed her with a good mind, and had given her a fair education, which was supplemented by tuition under Mary Lyon, of Holyoke Seminary, one of the first women preceptors of her time. She had a great desire to further continue her education, but was obliged to do it unaided. She began to teach a summer school when fifteen years of age, and worked in the cotton-mill in the winter, and thus was enabled to help her family, as well as to gratify her taste for reading and study.

In early life she educated a brother; and later she nearly supported him, and also assumed the whole expense of her aged mother's maintenance. And yet, in spite of these large drains upon her resources, she saved, solely from her own money, enough to start the library which bears her name, that her townspeople might enjoy the advantages she had so much desired. The Hon. Carroll D. Wright, United States Commissioner of Labor, was one of her pupils, and he delivered the address at the dedication of The Shedd Free Public Library, in 1882, speaking thus in praise of his well-beloved teacher:—

"The first school I ever attended was kept by her, in the front room of the store opposite the post-office. Her genial smile won the hearts of the children.... We longed for her coming, regretted her going. She wandered with us over the hills and fields, gave us instruction from her heart and mind, as well as from the books we used.... Her genial disposition lighted the pathway of many a boy and girl, and gave them glimpses of a mind and soul, which in themselves make her memory as fragrant as spring flowers."

Miss Shedd was not a prolific writer, and her contributions for *The Offering* were always of a serious nature. She spent no money on fine clothes nor ornaments; I remember her as a tall, spare, stooping woman, most plainly dressed in calico. We younger ones did not understand her, and were awed by her silence and reserve. But later some of us came to recognize her character as that of one studious, gentle, and self-sacrificing. She remains in my mind as one of the "solitary" among us. She died in Washington, N.H., April 5, 1867.

It is one of the coincidents of history, that, at about the same time Miss Shedd's money was given towards founding this library, another native of the same little town, Mr. Luman T. Jefts, who had also worked his way up and earned every cent of his money, should supplement Miss Shedd's gift by adding a sum large enough to erect a suitable library building to contain the books bought by her bequest.

And thus their names are linked together by their grateful townsmen, not only as benefactors of their kind, but also as two earnest and sincere persons who have struggled with adversity and narrow surroundings, have conquered, and fulfilled their cherished aim in life.

ELIZABETH EMERSON TURNER.

The subject of this sketch is one of the few of the early mill-girls who are still living; my acquaintance with her has been kept up since early girlhood, and our correspondence has been almost uninterrupted. She married Mr. Charles B. Sawyer, of Chicago, who died in 1896. Mrs. Sawyer has always retained her interest in the old factory days, and was and is proud of her connection with *The Lowell Offering.* In our letters, the prospect of publishing a book containing the material I had collected was often discussed; and she expressed her sympathy with the enterprise, saying,—

"I wish you would take up such a work as you allude to, in justice to those most interested, and to that class of girls in the Lowell mills. You are the one best fitted to do them full credit. I think the book would meet with a good sale, as labor is now becoming once more honorable and respectable.... We will see if our *Lowell Offering* cannot be made to live for many, *many* years to come; and be an object-lesson to the mill-girls of the present day."

Lizzie Turner was born in Lyme, N.H., Aug. 27, 1822. Her father, Jacob Turner, Esq., was a descendant in the sixth generation from Humphrey Turner, who came from England, and settled in Plymouth, Mass. He was for twenty years a justice of the peace in Lyme, and for two years a member of the New Hampshire Legislature. He lost his health before he reached middle life, and about the same time lost nearly all of his property by signing a note for a friend, who ran away to Canada, leaving him to pay the debt. In order to do this he sold his farm; and after paying the sum required, he had just five hundred dollars left. With this he went to Lowell, in 1833, where so many families who had lost their bread-winner had preceded him, and where the mother and children could assist in supporting the home. Mrs. Turner opened a boarding-house for operatives; her children, as fast as they were old enough, went to work in the mill; and thus the invalid father was well taken care of for the rest of his life.

Lizzie went into the mill to work at eleven years of age. Her school-days ended at fourteen, when she was just fitted for the high school, having worked at least two-thirds of the time in the factory; and after this her time and strength were needed to help support the family. She was one of the very earliest of the writers for *The Offering,* and she continued to be a contributor until Mr. Thomas ceased to be the editor. Her early recollections are very valuable, and all through these pages I have made free use of what information she has given me. She was just eighteen when she began her contributions; and her own account of her connection with the magazine and of its inception, will be of interest here. She says:—

"The whole plan of his Circle and *Offering* originated with Brother Thomas. I remember his saying one evening, after the reading of our papers, that there were many of the articles well worthy of publication, and that he should publish them in a magazine, to 'show what factory-girls could do.' ... I must tell you that I had never attempted writing anything but letters till Brother Thomas insisted that I *must* write something for the Circle, so that almost my first essays in composition were those articles."

Miss Turner was one of the paid contributors; she bought herself a mahogany bureau with some of this money, and that article of furniture she cherishes among her choicest possessions, as a most valuable memento of the old *Lowell Offering.*

I remember Lizzie Turner, when a young girl, as an intellectual factor among the contributors to *The Offering,* and also as a prominent worker in the Universalist Church. She was sprightly, vivacious, and universally popular. She was tall and graceful, had dark-brown hair, and star-bright eyes, which now, although she is a grandmother, have lost very little of their lustre, nor is her kindly and smiling expression diminished.

To illustrate the simplicity of dress of the mill-girls, before spoken of, and also to show how little thought they had of rivalling or of outdoing each other in matter of adornment, I venture to give the following as related to me by Mrs. Sawyer:—

"There were ten of us girl friends (the majority of whom wrote for *The Offering*) who one summer had each a purple satin cape for street wear. These were trimmed with black lace; and this, with a small-figured, light Merrimack print (or calico), constituted our walking costume. We had nothing better for Sunday wear; and as we walked along, sometimes all together, I am sure that it never occurred to one of us that we were not as well-dressed as any lady we met."

During the Civil War, Mrs. Sawyer was one of the most efficient among the many women in Chicago who worked for the soldiers and the country, and she has devoted much time and thought to the woman suffrage cause. She is a voter and an active member of The Illinois Woman's Alliance, of the Illinois Woman's Press Association, and of the Chicago Woman's Club.

Her sister, Abby D. Turner, was also one of the earliest writers for *The Offering;* her first contribution was written when she was sixteen years of age. She was married while in her teens to Mr. John Caryl. She has been a widow many years, and has been entirely devoted to her children and grandchildren.

CLEMENTINE AVERILL.

Among the "girl graduates" from the New England cotton-mill, there is one who, although not a writer for *The Offering,* yet deserves to be included in a book like this. This is Clementine Averill.

There was often doubt thrown upon the accounts of the superior mental, moral, and physical condition of the Lowell factory-girl; and at one time (in 1850) a Senator of the United States, named Clemens (of Alabama, I think), stated in Congress that "the Southern slaves were better off than the Northern operatives." Miss Averill, then at work in the Lowell mill, answered this person's allegation in a letter to the New York *Tribune,* as follows:—

LETTER FROM A FACTORY-GIRL
TO SENATOR CLEMENS.

Communicated for *The Weekly Tribune.*

LOWELL, *March* 6, 1850.

Mr. Clemens,—Sir, in some of the late papers I have read several questions which you asked concerning the New England operatives. They have been well answered perhaps, but enough has not yet been said, and I deem it proper that the operatives should answer for themselves.

1st, You wish to know what pay we have. I will speak only for the girls, and I think I am stating it very low when I say that we average two dollars a week beside our board. Hundreds of girls in these mills clear from three to five dollars a week, while others, who have not been here long, and are not used to the work, make less than two dollars. If my wages are ever reduced lower than that, I shall seek employment elsewhere.

2d, Children are never taken from their parents and put into the mill. What an idea! No person has a right to take a child from its parents, whether they be black or white, bond or free, unless there is danger of the child's suffering harm by remaining with its parents. Girls come here from the country of their own free will, because they can earn more money, and because they wish to see and know more of the world.

3d, One manufacturer will employ laborers dismissed by another if they bring a regular discharge and have given two weeks' notice previous to leaving.

4th, We never work more than twelve and a half hours a day; the majority would not be willing to work less, if their earnings were less, as they only intend working a few years, and they wish to make all they can while here, for they have only one object in view.

5th, When operatives are sick they select their own physician, and usually have money enough laid by to supply all their wants. If they are sick long, and have not money enough, those who have give to them freely; for let me tell you, there is warm-hearted charity here, as well as hard work and economy.

6th, I have inquired, but have not ascertained that one person ever went from a factory to a poor-house in this city.

7th, Any person can see us, who wishes to, by calling for us at the counting-room, or after hours of labor by calling at our boarding-places.

8th, The factory girls generally marry, and their husbands are expected to care for them when old. There are some, however, who do not marry, but such often have hundreds and thousands of dollars at interest; if you do not believe it, come and examine the bank-books and railroad stocks for yourself.

9th, We have as much and as good food as we want. We usually have warm biscuit, or nice toast and pie, with good bread and butter, coffee and tea, for breakfast; for dinner, meat and potatoes, with vegetables, tomatoes, and pickles, pudding or pie, with bread, butter, coffee and tea; for supper we have nice bread or warm biscuit, with some kind of sauce, cake, pie, and tea. But these questions seem to relate merely to our animal wants. We have all that is necessary for the health and comfort of the body, if that is all; and the richest person needs no more. But is the body all? Have we no minds to improve, no hearts to purify? Truly, to provide for our physical wants is our first great duty, in order that our mental faculties may be fully developed. If we had no higher nature than the animal, life would not be worth possessing; but we have Godlike faculties to cultivate and expand, without limit and without end. What is the object of our existence, if it is not to glorify God? and how shall we glorify him but by striving to be like him, aiming at the perfection of our whole nature, and aiding all within our influence in their onward progress to perfection? Do you think we would come here and toil early and late with no other object in view than the gratification of mere animal propensities? No, we would not try to live; and this is wherein consists the insult, both in your questions and in your remarks in the Senate; as though to provide for the body was all we had to live for, as though we had no immortal minds to train for usefulness and a glorious existence.

Let us see whether the "Southern slaves are better off than the Northern operatives." As I have said, we have all that is necessary for health and comfort. Do the slaves have more? It is in the power of every young girl who comes here to work, if she has good health and no one but herself to provide for, to acquire every accomplishment, and get as good an education as any lady in the country. Have the slaves that privilege? By giving two weeks' notice we can leave when we please, visit our friends, attend any school, or travel for pleasure or information. Some of us have visited the White Mountains, Niagara Falls, and the city of Washington; have talked with the President, and visited the tomb of him who was greatest and best. Would that our present rulers had a portion of the same spirit which animated him; then would misrule and oppression cease, and the gathering storm pass harmless by. Can the slaves leave when they please, and go where they please? are they allowed to attend school, or travel for pleasure, and sit at the same table with any gentleman or lady? Some of the operatives of this city have been teachers in institutions of learning in your own State. Why do your people send here for teachers if your slaves are better off than they? Shame on the man who would stand up in the Senate of the United States, and say that the slaves at the South are better off than the operatives of New England; such a man is not fit for any office in a free country. Are we torn from our friends and kindred, sold and driven about like cattle, chained and whipped, and not allowed to speak one word in self-defence? We can appeal to the laws for redress, while the slaves cannot. . . . And now, Mr. Clemens, I would most earnestly invite you, Mr. Foote, and all other Southern men who want to know anything about us, to come and see us. We will treat you with all the politeness in our power. I should be pleased to see you at my boarding-place, No. 61 Kirk Street, Boott Corporation. In closing, I must say that I pity not only the slave, but the slave-owner. I pity him for his want of principle, for his hardness of heart and wrong education. May God, in his infinite mercy, convince all pro-slavery men of the great sin of holding their fellow-men in bondage! May he turn their hearts from cruelty and oppression to the love of himself and all mankind! Please excuse me for omitting the "Hon." before your name. I cannot apply titles where they are not deserved.

CLEMENTINE AVERILL.

Miss Averill had many letters of congratulation upon this letter, from different parts of the country; and among them was one from the celebrated Quaker philanthropist, Isaac T. Hopper, who indorsed her words, as follows:—

NEW YORK, 3d mo., 19th, 1850.

My much esteemed friend, Clementine Averill,—I call thee so
on the strength of thy letter of the 6th inst., addressed to Senator
Clemens, which I have read in the *Tribune* of this morning with
much satisfaction. I ought to apologize for thus intruding upon
thy attention, being an entire stranger; but really I experienced
so much gratification on reading it that I could not resist the in-
clination I felt to tell thee how much I was pleased with it. The
information it contained, though perhaps not very gratifying to
the advocates of slavery, may be useful, as it so clearly exhibits
the wide difference there is between liberty and slavery, and it
shows the ignorance of the Southern people as to the condition of
the Northern operatives. I think Senator Clemens must have been
greatly surprised in reading thy letter, not only at its statement
of facts, but at the talent displayed by a "factory-girl" in answer-
ing his questions. Some years ago I attended a meeting appointed
at Lowell by a minister of the Society of Friends, at which it was
said there were about three hundred "factory-girls;" and I have
often expressed the satisfaction I felt in observing their independent and happy countenances and modest and correct deport-
ment. I saw nothing like gloom or despondency. Indeed, I think
in a general way they would not suffer by a comparison with the
daughters of the Southern slaveholders. I believe it would be
found, that, for refinement, intelligence, and for any qualification
that is requisite to constitute an agreeable companion, the "factory-girls" are not inferior to any class of women in the South,
notwithstanding the slurs that are often flung at them. It is surely
true, that as the benign spirit of the gospel pervades the minds
of men, slavery will be seen in its true character, and be finally
abolished from every community professing Christianity. I would
not limit the mercy of our beneficent Creator, but I am free to
confess that I am unable to see what claim a slaveholder can have
to the name of Christian. Avarice and an undue love of the world
blinds the eyes and hardens the hearts of many. The speech of
Daniel Webster, from whom the friends of liberty had a right to
expect much, has disappointed them, and has not pleased his
pro-slavery coadjutors. He has manifested himself to be a *time-
server,* a character not very desirable. If he had posessed as much
Christian principle and independence of mind as thy letter exhibits, he would have given utterance to sentiments that would
have gained him the applause of the wise and good, and have
been a lasting honor to himself. "With the talents of an angel a
man may make himself a fool." The subject of slavery is not new
to me. I have been instrumental in rescuing from the hand of the
oppressor some hundreds, and now in my declining years I can
look back upon those labors with unmingled satisfaction. I don't

know how to express my views of slavery better than in the language of John Wesley, "It is the sum of all villanies."

I am, with sincere regard,

Thy friend,

ISAAC T. HOPPER

I am indebted to Miss Averill's sister, Mrs. A. L. O. Stone of Cleveland, Ohio, for the means of communicating with her, and of obtaining some account of her life. Miss Averill's letter is as follows:—

VALRICO, FLA., Mar. 15, 1893.

Dear Mrs. Robinson,— ... I do not remember the date of my first entrance into the City of Spindles, but think it must have been in 1828; and it was the summer of 1830 that I was baptized in the Concord River, at the age of fifteen, and joined the First Baptist Church. I was born at Mt. Vernon, N.H., in the year 1815; so now I am seventy-eight.

About my Florida life, I must first tell the motive.

As you are aware, after the war, many were out of employment; and it was a great question, what should be done with them. I could see no better way than cooperative homes. Therefore, with two others, I started out to find a place, and set an example. I thought of some other places, but was much interested in Florida, having just read its history, and also my friends wished to come here. And, indeed, they did come before I was quite ready. A month later I came alone, December, 1877, just at Christmas time, and found the people here celebrating the day by firing guns. At Tampa I found one of my friends who had already selected land, and wished me to take an adjoining quarter-section. Had to come out from Tampa twelve miles to examine the land before I could enter my claim, then returned to register, and move my baggage out to a deserted log cabin in an old field by the side of the woods. The cabin had no floor but the bare ground, no window, and but one door. I spread a carpet of pine straw, and slept well."

She spent the winter in her forlorn log cabin, but in the spring she had a kitchen and bedroom, and soon after a split board floor. She "planted two hundred orange-trees, and cared for them two years." She made a living by "keeping transient boarders, by washing, needlework, baking bread and cakes to sell, and keeping house for various persons."

When her health began to fail, she made an agreement with one of her neighbors, Mr. Green, "to take care of me as long as I lived for half of my land; so the deed was made out and recorded, and I have only sixty acres for the industrial home." Later she writes:—

"I have never, for a moment, given up the idea of having an industrial home and school here sometime.

It is a pleasant location, having a small pond all under my control, with beautiful pine and oak trees all around it, and green slope down to the water. It is only ten minutes' walk to the station and post-office, and most of the way on my land. I gave right of way for a railroad through one corner, and yesterday gave one acre for a Baptist church.

I want a co-operative home here, established by homeless people who are willing to form a *Mutual Aid* Society. Then I can deed my land to the society, for a perpetual home here, as long as human beings need a home on this earth.

Perhaps you know some persons who might wish to join this home. If you do, please put me in communication with them, and they can ask all the questions they wish, and I will answer.

This station is fourteen miles east of Tampa, on the Florida Central and Peninsula Railroad.

Truly your friend,
CLEMENTINE AVERILL."

CHAPTER IX.

THE COTTON-FACTORY OF TO-DAY.

God has not gone to some distant star;
He's in the mill where the toilers are.

ANNA J. GRANNIS.

I should not feel that the whole purpose of this book had
been fulfilled unless I added a word in behalf of the factory
population of to-day.

It will probably be said that the life I have described cannot be repeated, and that the modern factory operative is
not capable of such development. If this is a fact, there
must be some reason for it. The factory of to-day might
and ought to be as much of a school to those who work
there as was the factory of fifty or sixty years ago. If the
mental status of these modern operatives is different, then
the opportunities of development should be adapted corres-
pondingly to their needs. The same results, perhaps, cannot be reached, because the children of New England ancestry had inherited germs of intellectual life. But is it not
also possible that the children of the land of Dante, of
Thomas Moore, of Racine, and of Goethe may be something
more than mere clods? I do not despair of any class of
artisans or operatives, because I believe that there is in them
all some germ of mental vigor, some higher idea of living,
waiting for a chance to grow; and the same encouragement
on the part of employers, the same desire to lift them to a
higher level, would soon show of what the present class of
operatives is capable.

What these poor people need is time, and a great deal of
help, before it can be decided what either they or their
descendants can make of themselves. Before an infallible
decision can be given, there must be, perhaps, two or three
generations of growth under free institutions, and under

employers who think of something besides coining the bodies and souls of their employees into dollars and cents.

No one can grow mentally, who has not time to read or to think, and whose life is a constant struggle to get enough food and clothing for himself and his family. Our working-people have their intellectual freedom, as well as the wage-question, to fight for, just as the ancestors of the early factory-operatives fought for their social and constitutional liberty. They will carry on the warfare in their own way; and if employers are wise they will try to do something practical to prevent strikes, riots, and labor-unions, which are the working-man's weapons of defence, and so to "lock the door before the horse is stolen."

Not long ago I was invited to speak to a company of the Lowell mill-girls, and to tell them something about my early life as a member of the guild. I was doubly willing to do this, as I was desirous of forming some estimate of the status of these successors of the early mill-girls.

About two hundred of them assembled in the pleasant parlors of the People's Club, and listened attentively to my story. When it was over, a few of them gathered around, and asked me many questions. In turn I questioned them,—about their work, their hours of labor, their wages, and their means of improvement. When I urged them to occupy their spare time in reading and study, they seemed to understand the necessity of it, but answered sadly: "We will try; but we work so hard, we tend so much machinery, and we are so tired." It was plainly to be seen that these operatives did not go to their labor with the jubilant feeling that the old mill-girls used to have; that their work was drudgery, done without aim and purpose; that they took little interest in it beyond the thought that it was the means of earning their daily bread. There was a tired hopelessness about them that I am sure was not often seen among the early mill-girls, and they had an underfed, prematurely old look.

The hours of labor are now less, it is true; but the operatives are obliged to do a far greater amount of work in a given time. They tend so many looms and frames that they have no time to think. They are always on the jump; and so have no opportunity to improve themselves. They are too weary to read good books, and too overworked to digest what they have read. The souls of many of these mill-girls seemed starved, and looked from their hungry eyes as if searching for mental food.

Why are they not fed? The means of education are not wanting. Public libraries are provided, and they have more leisure to read than the mill-girls of forty years ago. But they do not seem to know how to improve it. Their leisure only gives them the more time to be idle in; more time to waste in the streets, or in reading cheap novels and stories. It might almost be said that they are worse off than if they had longer hours, or did not know how to read, unless they can use to better advantage their extra time, or have the means of suitable education provided for them.

Let it not be understood that I would take from the operative or the artisan one of the chances of education. But I would have them taught how to use wisely those privileges, forced, we might almost say, on them and on their children. I would also have them taught how inwardly to digest what they are made to learn. The tools are given them; but as they are not taught how to use them, these prove but an additional weapon of defence against employers, and make them more discontented, and ready to listen to the political demagogue, or the so-called labor reformer. Then strikes ensue, which usually end, as the first Lowell one did, for the time being at least, in the success of the employer, rather than of the employee.

The solution of the labor problem is not in strikes, but, as another has said, in "bringing the question down to its simplest form, a practical carrying out of the golden rule; by the employer elevating the working-man in his own esteem by fair dealing, courteous treatment, and a constant appeal to his better side; and, on the other hand, in the working-man himself by the absence of malingering, by honest work, and a desire to further his employer's interests; and finally, to cement the two, a fair distribution of profits." "Not what we give, but what we share," is a good motto for the employers. Treat your employees as *you* would be treated, if, by the "accident of birth," loss of employment, or hard luck, *you* were in their condition. Treat them as if they, too, had something of God in them, and, like yourselves, were also His children. This is the philosophy of the labor question.

The factory population of New England is made up largely of American-born children of foreign parentage,— two-thirds it is estimated; as a rule, they are not under the strict control of the church of their parents, and they are too apt to adopt the vices and follies, rather than the good habits, of our people. It is vital to the interests of the whole community, that they should be kept under good moral influences; that they should have the sympathy, the help, of employers. They need better homes than they find in too many of our factory towns and cities, and a better social atmosphere, that they may be lifted out of their mental squalor into a higher state of thought and of feeling.

The modern system of overcrowding the mill-people is to be especially deprecated. In the old time, not more than two or three beds were put into one large bedroom, which was used only as a bedroom; but not long ago, according to an article in the *Springfield Republican* on "How Mill-People Live," it appears that Mr. H. R. Walker, agent of the Chicopee Board of Health, in his official report to the board, states that he found "twelve persons living and sleeping in a suite of two rooms, and sixteen persons living and sleeping in a tenement of four rooms." And in another block, owned by a "wealthy gentleman in that city," he found that "thirty-eight rooms were occupied by ninety-seven men, women, and children." Under such conditions, how can young people be brought up virtuously?

These are examples of overcrowding which I hope are not followed to any extent by the better class of manufacturing corporations; although there is reason to fear that overcrowding is getting to be the rule, rather than the exception.

The cotton-factories themselves are not so agreeable nor so healthful to work in as they used to be. Once they were light, well ventilated, and moderately heated; each factory-building stood detached, with pleasant sunlit windows, cheerful views, and fresh air from all points of the compass. But these buildings are now usually made into a solid mass by connecting "annexes," and often form a hollow square, so that at least one-half of the operatives can have no outlook except upon brick walls, and no fresh air but that which circulates within this confined space.

A year or two ago I revisited the dressing-room where I used to work, and found the heat so intense that I could hardly breathe; and the men who were working there (there were no women in the room) wore the scantiest of clothing, and were covered with perspiration.

The drying of the beams is done by hot air, though sometimes fans are added; the windows and doors are kept shut, except in very fine weather; and this makes an atmosphere unfit to breathe. My old overseer, who had had charge of one room for over forty years, told me that some time ago he had been obliged to change his occupation in the mill on account of the intense heat consequent on the introduction of this new method of drying the beams.

Nor are the houses kept clean and in repair as they used to be. In Lowell, when I last walked among the "blocks" where I lived as a child, I found them in a most dilapidated condition,—houses going to decay, broken sidewalks, and filthy streets; and contrasting their appearance with that of the "corporation" as I remember it, I felt as if I were revisiting the ruins of an industry once clean and prosperous. Would that I could say one word that would lead stockholders to see that it is not from out of such surroundings that the best dividends can be secured!

To one who has watched with sad interest the gradual decline of the cotton-factory industry in New England, and has marked the deterioration of its operatives, it has often seemed as if something might be done to restore this great factor in our national prosperity to its early influence and importance. Many schemes have been advanced by political economists, but, thus far, they have borne no fruit, and at this present writing, the Massachusetts Legislature itself has placed the whole subject in the hands of the Committee on Labor, who are to report on the several items submitted to its decision. While I would not venture here to discuss the various points on which this committee is to report, I cannot forbear calling attention to the first section, which relates to the "Dingley Tariff."

This section enquires, substantially, whether the Dingley tariff has had any influence in producing the present stagnation of the New England cotton industry. As a help to the solution of this question, or a suggestion at least, I will venture to quote from an article in the report of the Massachusetts Bureau of Statistics of Labor, on "The Age of Factory Establishments," where it is stated that "Quite one-half of the whole product of the State is made by manufactories which were in existence before 1860, and most of these establishments were founded in the industrial period following the beginning of the reduction of the tariff of 1828; and it can be said, with truth, that the great manufacturing industry of Massachusetts was planted in low-tariff times."

If this statement is correct, of which there can be no doubt, it has a significance worthy of attention, when we see the downward movement of the cotton industry under the present high-tariff. It was these "low-tariff times" that enabled working-people to buy goods that would last, which they cannot do in these days of "home production" shoddy, protected, as it is, by the Dingley tariff. And, without entering into the discussion, it would seem that a low tariff is certainly desirable for working-people, at least, since it enables them to get the best there is for their money, whether it be of foreign or domestic manufacture. An able writer has said: "The great trouble with the New England mills now is, that the people want a better class of goods which can compete with other textile products." This is certainly true, as applied to the buyer. A person of limited means can better afford to buy goods of foreign manufacture, no matter how high the tariff is. For woollens we look to England; for silks, to Lyons or Zurich; and lighter material must be of French manufacture. And the dealer says to you, as the best recommendation for the goods you wish to purchase, "It is *English,* or it is *French* goods, that I am showing you."

As for cheap American prints, who prefers to buy them nowadays? Certainly no woman who remembers with affection the good, pretty, durable, and *washable* old Merrimack print,—the old-time calico, that, when partly worn out, would still do for gowns and "tiers" for the children, or for comforters for the family beds. Gentlemen! mill-owners and managers! give us as good material as that we can buy of English and French manufacture, and we will wear no more dress-goods that are not of "home production," and will cheerfully pay you whatever price you may ask for them. This can certainly be done, with all your inventive genius, and you need no longer fear either foreign or Southern competition.

One more suggestion. It has often seemed that one great cause of the decline of the cotton industry is to be found in the change in the character of the operatives themselves. But could not some inducement be offered to call to this industry a better class of operatives, or to elevate a part of them towards the status of the old-time mill-girls? The factory-operatives of to-day are more like those of England, whom I have described, when the cotton manufacture first began in America. Then, mill-owners and stockholders knew that the daughters of New England would not become mill-girls under existing conditions, and unless they were sure of good wages and of being treated like human beings. This assurance was given; and the consequence was that they flocked from their homes, and so helped to build up an industry that was to give the first great impetus to the coming prosperity of the whole country. Could not this experiment be tried anew? There must be—there are—thousands of young women, all over New England, working for almost a pittance in stores and workshops, some of them twelve hours a day, subject to temptations that would never reach them in the cotton-factory,—women and girls who have no homes, who would gladly go to the factories, if a comfortable home, short hours, sure work, and steady wages were assured to them. Let the best

of them work by the job or piece, as far as possible; for
this shows, more than any other "reform in labor," where
the best class of operatives can be found, and the best result of their work can be secured. Why not try these or
some better experiments, and so uplift gradually the status
of the modern factory-operative?

These suggestions regarding a better class of goods and
a better class of operatives, if carried out, will involve sacrifice for a time on the part of the mill-owners and stockholders. But it is certainly better to sacrifice even a great
deal than it is to lose all; and there seems to be danger of
this if something radical and far-reaching cannot soon be
done to improve the present condition of our New England
cotton-factories and their operatives.

It is claimed that the factory is not a "philanthropic institution," and that corporations are not responsible for the
well-being of those they employ. But until Boards of Health
and Factory Inspectors can succeed in reforming the abuses
which exist among the mill-people, who but the corporation ought to be held responsible for the unwholesome
surroundings and the hard life which is undermining the
vitality and poisoning the blood of so large a portion of our
working-people?

"Labor is worship," says the poet. Labor is *education,*
is the teaching of the wise political economist. If factory-
labor is not a means of education to the operative of to-day,
it is because the employer does not do his duty. It is because he treats his work-people like machines, and forgets
that they are struggling, hoping, despairing human beings.
It is because, as he becomes rich, he cares less and less for
the well-being of his poor, and, beyond paying them their
weekly wages, has no thought of their wants or their needs.

The manufacturing corporation, except in comparatively
few instances, no longer represents a protecting care, a
parental influence, over its operatives. It is too often a soul-
less organization; and its members forget that they are
morally responsible for the souls and bodies, as well as for
the wages, of those whose labor is the source of their
wealth. Is it not time that more of these Christian men and

women, who gather their riches from the factories of the country, should begin to reflect that they do not discharge their whole duty to their employees when they see that the monthly wages are paid; that they are also responsible for the unlovely surroundings, for the barren and hopeless lives, and for the moral and physical deterioration of them and their children?

The cotton-factory gave the first impetus towards uplifting the social status of the working-men and working-women of New England, if not of the whole country. It should not be a cause of its decadence, as it certainly is in danger of becoming unless corporations can be induced to seriously consider whether it is better to degrade those who work for them to a level with the same class in foreign countries, or, to mix a little conscience with their capital, and so try to bring back, into the life of the factory operative of to-day, this "lost Eden" which I have tried to describe.